Chicken Scratchings
Fifty Inspirational Stories from a Mother Hen

By

Nancy Panko

Chicken Scratchings
Copyright © Nancy Panko

All rights reserved. No part of this book may be reproduced, stored, or transmitted by any means—whether auditory, graphic, mechanical, or electronic—without written permission of both publisher and author, except in the case of brief excerpts used in critical articles and reviews. Unauthorized reproduction of any part of this work is illegal and is punishable by law.

Kindle Direct Publishing
ISBN 9798852201935

This book is dedicated to a memorable patient, my family, and friends who are an endless font of material.

Thank you to all who helped make this book possible. I'm grateful for my patient husband who sometimes waited to have dinner while I was pecking away at the keyboard. Thank you to my peers in the NC Scribes Writing Circle who listened while I read every one of these stories and for offering critique for improvement. Thank you to my friends, Ellen Kennedy, Terry Hans, Dea Irby, Nancy Kimsey, Cynthia Wheaton, and Linda Hemby for reading my manuscript and/or helping to find solutions for glitches I encountered.

Table of Contents

Dedication
Acknowledgments
Foreword
Chapter 1   A Journey of Healing   page 2
Chapter 2   The Last Dance   page 6
Chapter 2   The Brown Glass Fish   page 10
Chapter 4   My Interstate Navigator   page 14
Chapter 5   Amazing Onyx   page 16
Chapter 6   Nun the Worse for Wear   page 19
Chapter 7   A Cast of Characters   page 22
Chapter 8   Mom's Macaroni Money   page 26
Chapter 9   Don't Drink the Poison   page 29
Chapter 10 Together Again   page 33
Chapter 11 No Room at the Inn   page 36
Chapter 12 St. Gerard and Me   page 39
Chapter 13 How to Upstage a Bride   page 42
Chapter 14 Stuck in the Ceiling   page 46
Chapter 15 Slips of the Tongue   page 49
Chapter 16 The Legacy of Mom's Christmas Stocking page 53
Chapter 17 Fleece Navidad   page 55
Chapter 18 I Woke Up!   page 58
Chapter 19 Perfect Timing   page 61
Chapter 20 Milk Money   page 63
Chapter 21 My January Gardenia   page 65
Chapter 22 A Purr-fect Spring Concert   page 67
Chapter 23 Good Girls Get Ice Cream   page 69
Chapter 24 Just Ask   page 71
Chapter 25 Held By an Angel   page 74
Chapter 26 A Perfect 10   page 77
Chapter 27 Guests for Christmas Break   page 81
Chapter 28 Hugs From Home   page 84
Chapter 29 What a Difference a Day Makes   page 86

Table of Contents

Unpublished Favorites

Chapter 30	About Your Canoe	page 95
Chapter 31	The Money Shot	page 97
Chapter 32	My Life as a Pink Ninja	page 100
Chapter 33	What a Hoot!	page 103
Chapter 34	A Note for the Teacher	page 106
Chapter 35	A Lasting Impression	page 108
Chapter 36	Stormin' Norman and Me	page 110
Chapter 37	Are Slips of the Tongue Contagious?	page 113
Chapter 38	Just Fourteen Days	page 116
Chapter 39	High Altitude Adventure	page 118
Chapter 40	Danger in the Doctors Office	page 122
Chapter 41	Our International Incidents	page 124
Chapter 42	Picture This	page 127
Chapter 43	The Story That Changed My Life	page 129
Chapter 44	Writing a Book About a Book	page 132
Chapter 45	Miracle on The Farm	page 135
Chapter 46	Grandma's Advice	page 137
Chapter 47	Miracle Maneuver	page 139
Chapter 48	January Christmas	page 142
Chapter 49	Never Take Normal For Granted	page 145
Chapter 50	Amorous Onyx	page 148
About the Author		page 151

Foreword

While working on my first novel, *Guiding Missal*, I wrote short stories to keep my skills sharp during periods of writer's block. My first story was published before my first novel. "A Journey of Healing" is about a life-changing miracle that occurred when I was a senior nursing student. *Chicken Soup for the Soul* accepted this first of many of my short stories for one of their books. Several others have been featured in *Woman's World* magazine, *Guideposts* Magazines, and *Reader's Digest*. Imagine my surprise when I found I had enough to make a book!

Each piece is a first-person account of an actual experience. The subjects vary from funny topics to serious ones. The publication information of the first twenty-nine chapters is noted at the end of each story. The remainder of the book is comprised of favorite pieces that have not yet been published. The reader will get a snapshot of my life, a glimpse of my family, and the depth of my faith. I hope you enjoy them.

Don't be ashamed of your story - it will inspire others!

1

A Journey of Healing

On a sunny July day, my younger brother Terry was killed as he attempted to cut down a tree. He died instantly of traumatic brain injury. In the blink of an eye, I no longer had a brother.

As I grieved, I found I wanted to pay tribute to his life by fulfilling my childhood dream. I enrolled in nursing school, got good grades and made the Dean's List. In my junior year, I began carpooling with Jeanne, one of the Intensive Care Unit (ICU) instructors. Driving fifty miles a day, we shared family stories. I explained how Terry's death affected my decision to return to school and how fearful I was even thinking about treating a patient with a traumatic brain injury. She listened intently and seemed sympathetic.

The day before our senior year Intensive Care clinical experience, Jeanne—my instructor and carpool friend—assigned me a traumatic head injury patient. Thinking of what lay ahead, I prayed silently for help. I HAD to give this patient the best care possible.

Upon entering the ICU, I learned that my patient was in surgery, having his second operation to relieve pressure from a blood clot on his brain. The doctors had given him little chance of survival. Terry had no chance at all, but this guy did. He was still here, fighting for his life, and I was going to do everything in my power to help him. I prayed for my patient and his family in the waiting room.

That afternoon and evening, I studied the patient's chart. His name was Sam, he was nineteen years old, the youngest child of a large family, and his accident was eerily similar to Terry's. Sam worked for a tree trimming company. While strapped in his safety harness, a falling limb hit him in the head. He hung upside down in the tree for nearly an hour before being extricated. He suffered a fractured skull with a large blood clot in his brain. A device was in place to relieve and measure the pressure inside his skull. A ventilator helped him breathe, he had arterial lines, IVs and a urinary catheter. He had been given last rites—twice.

The next day, just after dawn, I saw Sam for the first time. His head was swathed in bandages; he was unresponsive and his tall frame was motionless in the bed.

My knees were weak, but I knew every detail of his physical condition, medications, procedures and the readings on his monitors. In ICU, the details can mean the difference between life and death.

I can do this, I reassured myself. All my years of training and hard work came down to this day and this patient. I laid my hand on Sam's arm.

"Good morning, Sam. I'm your nurse for today. My name is Nancy." I told him the day of the week, the date, the time, and what the weather was. I chattered on while gently caring for him. There was no response.

In the ICU waiting room, I approached a tired-looking woman and introduced myself to Sam's mother. She told me all about Sam and the family. I asked her to bring a small radio to play his favorite music and family pictures to tape in easy-to-spot places around his cubicle. I shared my plan to gently stimulate Sam in the hopes of helping him come out of the coma. She was pleased that she could help.

Each day we carried out the plan. I talked to Sam and played his favorite music. While completing all my nursing duties, I told him about the leaves changing colors and the apples and cider for sale along the roadside. There was no response. It was hard to see this young man remain so still.

One day, as I struggled to put one of his heavy, long legs into his pajama bottoms, I said, "Sam, it would be great if you could help me. Can you lift your leg?" His leg rose five inches off the bed. I tried to remain calm. "Thank you, Sam. Can you raise the other leg?" He did! He could hear and follow commands, he had bilateral movement, but still, he had not regained consciousness or opened his eyes.

The next morning, I was told that during the night Sam had started breathing against the ventilator. As I entered his cubicle, I put my hand in his and told him I was there for the day. Sam squeezed it! I grabbed his other hand and asked him to squeeze again. He obeyed. By the afternoon, he was breathing totally on his own and I was able to take the breathing tube out of his throat. He no longer required the ventilator. It was a miracle.

Still, his eyes remained closed. As I worked with Sam the next day, he turned his head from side to side to follow my voice wherever I was. I brought his mother into the unit. "Sam," I said, as his face turned towards me, "your mom is here." A tear slid down his cheek. "Sam," I repeated as I came to stand behind his mother, "your mom is here. Please open your eyes." We watched him struggle to lift his lids. His eyes fluttered open, he looked toward the sound of my voice. "Sam," I said, "look at your mom." Suddenly, recognition dawned in his eyes, and he began to cry. I partially lowered the bed side rail for a long-awaited mother and son embrace.

Sam continued to improve rapidly and was soon discharged from ICU to the rehabilitation unit.

A few weeks later, while walking through the rehabilitation unit, I heard someone call my name. It was Sam's mother. We hugged. She was smiling. I saw a tall, handsome young man standing next to her. His previously shaved head had grown into a crew cut, beginning to hide the many scars.

"Hi Sam, how are you?" I said.

He cocked his head and spoke. "Your voice sounds so familiar."

The lump in my throat only allowed me to respond, "I was one of your nurses in ICU."

His words came out haltingly, "You are Nancy. My mother told me all about you."

Here was a true miracle standing before me. For two weeks, my life was intertwined with Sam's as we each experienced miraculous healing.

One day, while Jeanne and I were driving to school, I gathered the courage to ask her why she blindsided me by assigning me a traumatic head injury patient when she knew my story. She explained that she believed in my nursing skills and even more so in my character. She wanted me to face my fear while she was there to watch over and support me. I was touched by her kindness.

A few months later, I received flowers from Sam's family. The card read, "To our Angel!" Sharing this journey of healing, Sam and I definitely had someone watching over us.

Christian Women's Voice Magazine
Published 2014

Chicken Soup for the Soul - Find Your Inner Strength
101 Empowering Stories of Resilience, Positive Thinking, and Overcoming Challenges
Published 2014

Guideposts Magazine - Angels on Earth
Published 2016

2

The Last Dance

My parents married on June 27, 1942, in a beautiful stone church in upstate New York. The bride was seventeen, the groom twenty. After promising to love and to cherish until parted by death, they danced at the reception. They kept these promises and continued to dance for seventy years.

During their courtship and their entire married life, they enjoyed big band music. They were beautiful dancers, commandeering the floor with style and grace. We kids grew to love the sound of Glenn Miller and Tommy Dorsey, conjuring up images of our parents gazing into each other's eyes as they glided across the floor.

I was the oldest, followed by my brother Terry and three sisters Judy, Gail, and Joni. We grew up in a house filled with love and a strong sense of family. The radio was always playing music, and at the first strains of Glenn Miller's "In The Mood" or "Sentimental Journey" our parents rolled the living room rug back. We kids sat cross-legged on the sofa to watch the magic happen. The hardwood floors of the farmhouse became a grand ballroom as we watched them move as one. Each of us grew up loving music of all types and dancing of all styles.

Tragedy struck in 1976 when our brother Terry was killed in a horrible accident. He was only thirty and left behind a young wife and three-year-old daughter.

Having suffered rheumatic fever and subsequent heart damage as a child, Mom began to have cardiac problems. Three months after Terry's death, our mother had open-heart surgery at age fifty. She recovered without a single complication while grieving the loss of her only son.

She had heart surgeries again in 1992 and 2002, and Dad was her devoted caregiver. By her side day and night, he was her dance partner and referred to her as his Princess.

Despite health issues, Mom and Dad's dancing days weren't over. Their love for big band music continued, but they could only hold each other and sway in time to the music. They longed to twirl around the floor as in earlier years, but settled for the gentle moves.

When my father, who had always been the hearty one, got sick, we steeled ourselves. The doctors at Duke Medical Center diagnosed aortic stenosis, and at the age of ninety, Dad had open-heart surgery. For two days, Mom didn't leave his side. She looked drawn and pale. We knew Mom was tired, but we didn't know she was in kidney failure.

On the third day of Dad's post-op recovery, eighty-seven-year-old Mom was hospitalized. Our hearts were heavy. It was the end of an era. Despite the seriousness of their conditions, the Lord was not done with them. Their love and devotion would show the rest of the family the meaning of the words "for better, for worse, in sickness and in health."

A week later, both parents, weak and tired, were discharged to my sister Judy's home. Timing was critical for the surprise we planned. I arrived with Mom and got her settled in bed when Judy came through the door with Dad. With her assistance, he walked to the bedroom.

Judy steadied Dad as he paused, gazing at Mom in their bed. He bent over and kissed Mom on the cheek. "Is it really you, Princess?"

She reached up with her hand and cupped it around his head. "Yes, it's me. Are you really here?"

He answered by getting in bed with her. They nestled into each other's arms as Judy and I stood in the doorway crying. We didn't know how long we'd have either of them, but we knew we'd do our best to keep them together.

Six weeks later, Mom had a setback and died after a few days in the hospital. The family was devastated. It was as if we had the wind knocked out of us.

Living without her was a struggle for Dad. They had been married seventy years. A year after Mom's death, Dad fell ill and began his downward spiral. Two months later, as he lay dying, he turned to me and announced in a weak voice. "I'm going to be with your mother for our anniversary on June 27th. We are going on a cruise and we'll dance to big band music."

It was one of the last conversations we had. He passed peacefully the evening of June 26th, right on schedule for their anniversary the next day.

Mom and Dad were both cremated. They requested that their ashes be combined and spread on my brother's grave and then be committed to the waters in front of our summer vacation house. We honored their request but added touches we thought they would both love.

For the entire four-day weekend we honored their memory. We gathered as sisters and our husbands along with Terry's widow, experiencing the closeness that our parents had instilled in us.

Having combined Mom and Dad's cremated remains, we returned them to a heart-shaped biodegradable box provided by the funeral home. We sealed it shut with superglue, as directed, preparing for a water burial.

On a beautiful sunny day in early September, we left the dock in two kayaks and a fishing boat, slowly moving into the deeper water of the bay. Our youngest sister Joni paddled one of the kayaks, our brother-in-law Jeff accompanied her in the other. The rest of us were in the boat. Mark turned his stereo system on. Strains of "Moonlight Serenade" followed by "Sentimental Journey" wafted across the water.

Gently resting the container on the gunwale of the boat, each sister placed a hand on the heart-shaped box for the last time. We said a prayer as we prepared to commit our parents' ashes to the body of water they loved so dearly.

Joni, sitting low in her kayak, received the box and reverently placed it in the water. It began to sink in exactly four minutes, as the directions said it would. We watched until it sank out of sight. "Sentimental Journey" was into the chorus.

Suddenly, two identical whirlpools rose to the surface of the water. Side by side the whirlpools moved in perfect syncopation across the water toward the main house. All of us watched in stunned silence as tears streamed down our faces. We looked at each other and said, "Did you see that?"

Dad had told me they were going on a cruise and would be dancing to big band music. He was right. At that moment, each one of us knew it was a sign from our beloved parents, a joyous sign of a couple in love gliding across the surface of a new dance floor in their last dance.

Chicken Soup for the Soul - Hope & Miracles
101 Inspirational Stories of Faith, Answered Prayers, and Divine Intervention
Published 2015

3

The Brown Glass Fish

My sister Judy and I stood by our father's bedside as he took his last breath. He passed away in the early evening, surrounded by people who loved him.

He had fought the good fight for two months. Judy and I spent hours with him every day. Our conversations covered many topics, not the least of which was his growing faith. He had one son who predeceased him and four living daughters. Dad was very close with Terry's widow, Laura. Each of his girls got to spend precious time with him except for Laura, who was struggling with a debilitating illness and unable to travel to North Carolina from her home in New Jersey.

Remembering Gail and Joni's approaching birthdays, Dad was relieved when I offered to shop for him. I asked if he also wanted me to get something for Laura, whose birthday was a few weeks later.

He responded, "No, we have time to do that."

We didn't have time; we just didn't know it.

When Gail and Joni arrived from Pennsylvania, Dad presented each of them with a pair of lovely earrings and what we girls call a "lumpy" card—a greeting card that causes a lump in the throat. It was a tearful, tender moment.

He died two weeks later, on a Wednesday evening.

That Friday night, I lay in bed trying to fall asleep. My head was filled with thoughts of Dad. I thought, "Thank God my sisters Judy, Gail, Joni, and I were able to spend time with him before he died. We will treasure those memories."

Laura's birthday was approaching, and I asked the heavens, "Dad, what would you want me to get for her?"

Between wakefulness and slumber, I heard my father's voice clearly, "The brown glass fish in the little brown box."

It was definitely Dad's voice.

Aloud, I said, "What?"

Again, he repeated, "The brown glass fish in the little brown box."

This was too much. I sat up and swung my legs over the side of the bed. I had heard it loud and clear, but what did it mean? I got out of bed and slid my feet into my slippers. I walked to the room where Dad had slept and stood in the doorway, sweeping the room with my eyes. I saw nothing resembling a little brown box. I backed out into the hall and went into his bathroom. Again, nothing that looked like a little brown box. I walked into Dad's TV room, looking from one side of the room to the other. My eyes landed on three trunks stacked in the corner of the room.

The top trunk could look like a little brown box to someone with macular degeneration. To confirm that, I sat in Dad's recliner in front of the flat-screen TV and looked to my right. With only peripheral vision, Dad would have seen that as a little brown box.

I stood up, walked to the stack, and picked up the little trunk. I couldn't even remember what was kept in it.

Opening the lid, I saw that the top trays were filled with small seashells and a variety of jewelry hardware. No sign of any brown glass fish. I removed the top tray and saw larger items in the bottom. Moving them around, my hand found an unopened package. Inside, I found a colorful enameled glass fish pendant. Of course! I vaguely remembered buying it several years ago. By then, it was 1 a.m. I closed up the small trunk and lay the package containing the glass fish on the sewing machine.

I told myself I'd look at it more closely in the morning. Suddenly, despite being very alert just minutes ago, I felt incredibly sleepy, like I could barely make it back to bed.

In the morning, I awoke well-rested. I got up and headed for Dad's TV room to get the pendant. It was a glass fish but it wasn't brown as Dad had insisted.

I put the package in my bathrobe pocket, went to the kitchen, and poured myself some coffee. While sitting in the breakfast nook sipping my morning jolt of caffeine, I opened the package and admired the workmanship of the enameled glass fish. The sun was streaming in the window, foretelling a gorgeous summer day. Impulsively, I held the fish pendant up to the light and couldn't believe my eyes. It looked totally brown, the colors of the enamel weren't apparent at all. It was simply a brown glass fish when held up to the light. This is what Dad wanted to give Laura for her birthday.

I created a lovely necklace with the glass fish pendant and sent it to Laura from Dad. When she received the package, she called me.

"Can I open it now?"

"Hey, it's not your birthday yet."

"I'm impatient."

"Okay. You can open it. I can't wait to hear your reaction. Dad wanted you to have this. After you open it, call me and I'll tell you the whole story."

Five minutes later, I received a text. Laura wrote, "I will call you as soon I stop crying."

I knew then that it had a powerful message for her from Dad.

Ten minutes later, the phone rang.

"Tell me the story," she said.

I related the entire incident.

She replied. "When your brother was killed, you mom and dad literally and figuratively held me up and held me together. I had lost my husband, and they had lost their only son."

By this time, we were both crying.

Laura continued, "Dad took me fishing every chance we got. It was just the two of us, sitting in a gently rocking boat in the warm sun. As we fished, we reminisced about Terry and shared our grief. I know what Dad wanted to tell me with this gift. He and Terry are together."

Chicken Soup for the Soul - Angels and Miracles
101 Inspirational Stories about Hope, Answered Prayers, and Divine Intervention
Published 2016

Guideposts Magazine - Mysterious Ways
Published 2017

4

My Interstate Navigator

Zooming down Pennsylvania Interstate 80, I was heading east to Allentown. The beautiful lush green mountains loomed above both sides of the highway. Every few miles a farm appeared nestled among the rolling hills. It was a beautiful day with no weather issues and very little traffic.

But I couldn't really enjoy it. I was rushing to Lehigh Valley Hospital, where my mom had suffered a setback. She had called me at work two hours before, crying that she needed me. As her daughter and a nurse, I couldn't ignore her plea. I left work, drove home to throw some clothes into a suitcase, and let my husband know where I was going and why.

In an effort to calm my mother, I had promised her, "I'll be right there." What was I thinking? It was a three-hour trip.

Ahead I saw a large tractor-trailer laden with lumber. The load was held in place with multiple straps. As I looked at the trailer, I started to feel uneasy.

A voice said clearly, "Those straps are going to break."

"What?" I asked incredulously.

The voice elaborated. "The straps are going to break and that lumber is going to spill onto the road."

"Holy Mother of God!" I thought, panicked at what the voice was telling me. I was a few car lengths behind the truck and we were both moving at about seventy miles per hour.

The voice urged, "Pass him. Get away from him. Do it now."

I obeyed, but when I pulled into the passing lane, the truck accelerated. I increased my speed enough to overtake the truck and kept an eye on the hazardous load.

Horrified, I watched as the straps holding the stacks of lumber in place started snapping, one by one, and twirling around uselessly in the air. Everything seemed to be happening in slow motion. When the third strap broke, the lumber started to shift.

The voice said authoritatively, "Pedal to the metal; get away from him as fast as you can."

I didn't question the voice. I floored it.

As my small sedan pulled away from that big truck, I watched the scene unfold in my rearview and side view mirrors. The stacks of wood rotated sideways and cascaded onto the road. The first pieces missed the back of my car by a few feet. I saw the truck slow down and could see the look of horror on the driver's face as he realized what was happening. He could clearly see the lumber slide off his truck onto both eastbound lanes of Route 80.

I safely pulled away and my speed returned to normal as I viewed the spectacle in the rearview mirror. I watched as the trucker brought his vehicle to a stop.

I offered up a prayer of thanks for having heard the voice. There was no doubt in my mind that God was my navigator on the interstate that day.

Chicken Soup for the Soul - Angels and Miracles
101 Inspirational Stories about Hope, Answered Prayers, and Divine Intervention
Published 2016

Guideposts Magazine - Mysterious Ways
Published 2017

Woman's World Magazine
Publish 2020

5

Amazing Onyx

She was the prettiest Lab puppy we had ever seen, and the whole family immediately fell in love with her. We named her Onyx because of her thick, shiny black coat. She spent her first vacation with us when she was only ten weeks old. She had her first bath and swim in the St. Lawrence River. We had no clue that this amazing little ball of fur would end up being our hero.

As she got older, Onyx learned to fish. Standing perfectly still while waiting patiently in the clear, shallow water, she'd carefully watch smallmouth bass dart around her feet until she dunked her head underwater and caught one in her mouth without leaving a tooth mark. We taught her the concept of "catch and release."

Onyx was also a skilled hunting dog, never afraid to show up her larger, more mature counterparts. She would not hesitate to crash through the ice on a tributary of the Chesapeake Bay to retrieve waterfowl. She braved the defensive posture of a hissing, wounded goose to bring it back to her master. She loved being by her master's side, whether in a duck blind or riding in the front seat of a pickup truck.

Onyx smiled. It was a people-like smile, but it intimidated those who didn't know her. Strangers misunderstood the showing of her teeth until they saw the upturn of her lips. If she was happy and content, Onyx smiled.

When she wasn't hunting, Onyx enjoyed all our family activities. On hot summer days, when the humidity was oppressive,

Onyx enjoyed floating on the river with us in her own inner tube. She smiled while showing off her perfect balance.

One hot day, our eighteen-year-old daughter, Margie, announced she wanted to swim across the bay. No one in the family was free to go with her. The unwritten rule, regardless of swimming ability, was to have a buddy in the water with you, especially when swimming the width of the bay. Margie never argued about that rule even though she had been an accomplished member of a swim team for many years.

Her father said, "Take Onyx with you."

Having heard her name, Onyx roused from a nap, ready for action.

"Go with Margie," he said to the dog.

Margie beckoned to the dog with a hand signal. Onyx trotted to the water next to her.

They entered the chilly river together and swam side-by-side across the bay. I watched from the deck as they reached the sandbar on the far shore.

Margie stood and smoothed her wet hair back from her face. They rested a few minutes before diving into the water for the return trip.

I felt uneasy for some reason and continued to watch the pair swim side by side. Then I heard Margie struggle, calling out, "I have a cramp!"

Onyx began swimming circles around her, sensing her distress. Margie was trying to massage the cramp but began struggling in the water. I ran to the dock, got into the rowboat, and started untying the ropes wrapped around the dock cleats.

Onyx knew Margie was in trouble. She came up behind and to Margie's side, poking her head underneath the girl's right arm. Margie grabbed onto Onyx's collar.

Onyx began digging deep, slicing through the water with her webbed paws, swimming with every ounce of strength to bring Margie back to the dock.

Watching the drama, I realized I didn't need to take out the boat. I simply waited until the pair approached me. Calling out encouragement to both my daughter and my dog, as they got closer I extended an oar to Margie. She grabbed it and held onto it with one arm while the other gripped our heroic dog's collar. Onyx brought our girl to the safety of the shore where her father and I could help her get out of the water.

Onyx jumped up onto the dock and shook vigorously several times. After Margie was wrapped in a large towel, she lowered herself to the grassy front lawn to rest. Onyx eagerly ran to her, covering her face with sloppy dog kisses. Wrapping our arms around both of them, we praised our amazing dog and gently tousled Margie's wet hair. Everyone was grateful for their safe return to shore.

Later in the afternoon, Onyx got an extra treat. She didn't quite understand all the fuss; she just wanted to jump off the dock again and swim around in the bay.

During subsequent family gatherings at the summerhouse, we'd reminisce and lift our glasses to our amazing Onyx and the day she became a hero.

Chicken Soup for the Soul - My Very Good, Very Bad Dog
101 Heartwarming Stories about our Happy, Heroic & Hilarious Pets
Published 2016

6

Nun the Worse for Wear

While dusting the furniture in the living room, I realized we never used this room anymore. I had long bemoaned not having enough space for our dining room table and here was an entire area adjacent to the kitchen that would be perfect! It was filled with living room furniture that was as good as new because we never sat on it. Surely, someone else could put this beautifully upholstered, three-piece sectional with two cherry tables to good use.

My husband, the keeper of all things, would need a solid explanation. I had one. He would need justification. I had that too.

When George came home from work that night, I poured him a cold beer, and he sat down to read the newspaper while I put the finishing touches on dinner. When he was sufficiently relaxed, I announced we were ready to eat. We sat down at the table. The stage was set, and I was on.

"I'd like to sell our living room furniture," I announced.

"Which living room?" he asked, "And why?"

"The one upstairs, in the next room. We never use that furniture anymore. We always gravitate to the family room downstairs. I'd like to convert this larger room to a dining area so I can put the leaves in the table when we entertain. We have the breakfast bar in the kitchen for the four of us in the morning."

He pondered those thoughts and surprised me by saying, "You're right. What's your plan."

I shared my idea of putting an ad in the newspaper and on Craigslist. George was happy to give me free rein, leaving the planning and execution entirely up to me. So I placed the ad.

I didn't realize how emotionally attached I was to this living room set until the first prospective buyer came to take a look. They talked about reupholstering and taking it apart and weren't sure they liked the wood. I felt my stomach churn. I wanted to yell, "That's solid cherry!" and I was glad when they left, saying they needed to think about it. I also needed time to think because something was telling me to hold off selling this furniture.

Several nights later, I had a vivid dream. Of nuns. They were the nuns in the convent across town who worked at the Catholic elementary school our son attended. In my dream, they urgently needed a new couch. We delivered our furniture to them with our pickup truck, and a few strong men placed it in their living room. I saw the sisters run their hands over the unblemished upholstery while they marveled at the lovely cherry tables. I remember being happy to know the set was going to a good home.

Over breakfast, I shared my dream with George. He looked at me, smiled, and gently patted my cheek. He said, "It'll be okay." I'm sure he thought I would need counseling after letting the furniture go.

As soon as he left for work, I called the convent. I spoke with one of the nuns and asked if I could drop by that afternoon. She said they would have the teapot on and looked forward to seeing me.

When I arrived at the convent, I was greeted by the principal of the school. "Come in, come in, we've been waiting for your visit."

She ushered me into their living room. "Please have a seat," she said. "But be careful on that old sofa, it has a spring poking through it and can hurt if you sit on the wrong spot." Sure enough, when I sat down, I felt the offending spring prodding me to move to the right.

The sisters and I talked over tea and I addressed the reason for my visit, the living room suite for which I was trying to find a home. I described the design, size and color and asked if they thought they could use it.

The principal put her hand up to her mouth. "We've been praying for a way to replace the old sofa, but I'm afraid we can't afford to buy anything for the house."

"I don't want to sell it to you, I want to give it to you."

The sisters clapped their hands with unabashed glee as they praised the Lord for an answer to their prayers. It was just like my dream. Now I knew why I wasn't supposed to sell that furniture!

The deal was done, and we set a date for delivery. I reassured the sisters that we would arrange to have the manpower to unload the set, place it in their living room and remove the old sofa.

Later that week, our living room sectional was taken to its new home in the convent. The nuns were delighted and I was relieved. I explained to them how badly I wanted a good home for our very first furniture on which as newlyweds, we had cuddled while watching TV and later had held our children as we read stories aloud.

As George and I left the convent, the wise and kind sisters called out from the doorway, "You have visiting rights for as long as you need!"

Chicken Soup for the Soul - The Joy of Less
101 Stories About Having More by Simplifying Our Lives
Published 2016

7

A Cast of Characters

The first week of September gave us a beautiful late summer evening that made us glad to be alive. I wanted to be outside but sat at the kitchen table studying for a biochemistry exam. George was relaxing, reading the newspaper. Our fourteen-year-old daughter was attending the first high school football game of the season, and our seven-year-old son, Tim was in the front yard playing soccer with a friend. Suddenly, a blood-curdling scream outside had us jumping up and racing toward the sound. My gut churned upon hearing an agonizing howl of pain coming from our child.

George and I burst through the screen door, running toward our boy lying on the ground screaming, "My leg, my leg!"

Rushing to his side, I cradled his head and told him to lie still and not move. Tears streamed down his face as he reached toward his contorted leg.

"Call 9-1-1," I said to my husband. I was sure Tim's leg was broken.

At the first sound of sirens and sight of flashing lights, many neighbors flooded into the street. The ambulance and EMTs pulled into our driveway and promptly got to work. They splinted the lower half of Tim's body and moved him onto a stretcher.

Our neighbor, a nurse, approached and offered to call the surgeon she worked with to meet us in the ER.

Gratefully, we said yes. Tim was loaded into the ambulance which left for the hospital with lights and sirens. We followed in the car.

The ride was short, and the surgeon was waiting for us. Technicians whisked our frightened seven-year-old off to X-ray. George and I trailed alongside, holding his hand.

Minutes later, I stood next to the doctor as we looked at the films. "A spiral fracture of the femur is serious business." I could see exactly what he meant. There were a good three inches between the ends of the broken bones.

I faced the doctor. "What does this mean as far as treatment and hospitalization?"

"He'll need a pin in his leg and then two weeks in traction. When the bones are aligned, I'd put him in a hip spica cast."

"What's that?"

"It's a little smaller than a full-body cast, starting just under his rib cage, extending to his toes on the fractured leg and to his knee on the uninjured one. A stabilizing bar will be attached as part of the cast to keep his legs in alignment."

I felt weak in the knees, and my mind was racing. I was in my first full year of nursing school twenty-six miles away. The only prayer I had of staying in school was to have Tim transferred to an orthopedic specialist at the hospital where I was training. I could stay with him when I wasn't in class, do my homework in his room and spend nights in the nurse's residence. The surgeon respected my wishes and gave the order for the transfer.

That short-term plan would suffice as long as he was hospitalized, but what would we do when he was discharged in that hip spica thing? George calmly reassured me we'd take one day at a time.

When our parents heard what happened, they said, "What do you need? And how soon do you need us to come?" We were relieved at their generous offer to help and set up a tentative schedule, to be firmed up as soon as we had a discharge date.

Two weeks later, we were given instructions for home care. Two people had to turn Tim every two hours because he was no longer a featherweight little boy, but a large, bulky plaster boy. At all costs, we could not jostle the metal skeletal pin apparatus protruding from the cast. We had to make sure he was adequately hydrated to help prevent blood clots due to his inactivity. He had cutouts in the cast to allow for bodily functions, using a bedpan and a urinal. We borrowed a mechanic's creeper so we could place him on his stomach to play. Elevated on pillows to keep the metal apparatus from touching the floor, Tim easily pulled himself around on the ball-bearing casters while he maneuvered his little cars and Army men. We alternated him between a sofa bed downstairs during the day and his own bed at night.

Our parents lived with us and cared for Tim for three weeks. Everyone had a tutorial on how to care for the boy in the cast. George came home for long lunches to pitch in. However, weeks loomed ahead where we had no help.

When our wonderful neighbors heard there was a possibility I'd have to leave school to take care of Tim one, in particular, became a lifesaver, setting up a schedule of volunteers to help during the workweek. A nurse herself, Lynne was eager to assist. She was a godsend. Words can never express how grateful we were for her help. She brought a red stake wagon, which was padded with many pillows so she could pull Tim around the neighborhood on nice days. She set up a chaise lounge in the shade of the front porch with, you guessed it, lots of pillows, and Tim could color or read books.

For three weeks, my neighbors covered Monday through Friday so I didn't have to take a leave of absence from school. My heart burst with thankfulness for their sacrifice and kindness.

After six weeks in the cast, Tim was admitted to the hospital to have the contraption removed and begin physical therapy to learn to walk all over again. I stayed in the nurse's residence each night until he came home walking with a tiny walker. He was not allowed back to school until he could manage on crutches. When that goal was reached, George drove him to school in the morning, and Lynne picked him up in the afternoon. Both kids got home about the same time, and Margie supervised her little brother until I got home at 4 p.m. It was a team effort.

One afternoon in the first week of December, three months to the day after Tim's accident, I came through the door to see my two beautiful children sitting at the table having a snack. "We have a surprise for you, Mom. Close your eyes."

"Okay, they're closed," I said.

Several seconds passed. "Open your eyes now, Mom."

I opened my eyes to see both kids grinning from ear to ear. Tim was standing unassisted and walked slowly toward me. I began to cry as he reached out his arms for the best hug ever.

Three years later, I graduated from nursing school. It humbles me to know my achievement would not have been possible without the kindness and sacrifice of family and friends to get us through a most difficult time.

Chicken Soup for the Soul - My Kind of America
101 Stories about the True Spirit of Our Country
Published 2016

8

Mom's Macaroni Money

We didn't have a lot of money while I was growing up, but one would never have guessed. Mom and Dad tended a large garden that yielded bountiful crops of vegetables. They nurtured a flock of chickens that provided us with fresh eggs. Mom learned to sew, and made our clothes. She honed her cooking and baking skills by watching my grandmother next door, and soon rivaled her teacher in pie baking.

As the four of us—one boy and three girls— got older, Mom yearned to give us an allowance. After reading one of the hand-me-down women's magazines from Grandma, Mom found a way to do it.

She instituted a unique system of paying an allowance to each of us without using money. I was eleven, my brother Terry was nine, and our two little sisters were five and three. Each of us was capable of doing something to help Mom. She couldn't wait to try this innovative reward system on her children.

Each time we completed our assigned chores, helped her around the house, or gave a hand to a younger sibling, Mom wrote in a notebook she carried in her apron pocket. Four empty canning jars labeled with our names sat on the kitchen counter. Payment came in the form of elbow macaroni, each piece of pasta equivalent to a nickel. Mom recorded the macaroni transactions in her little notebook.

Once a week, Mom called us together, and as we danced around her, she placed the macaroni we had earned in our hands.

We had the pleasure of depositing the little noodles in our jars. The younger girls, Judy and Gail, had to be reminded not to eat their allowance, as they both had a fondness for uncooked pasta.

At the end of the week, we got to spend a portion of our allowance by shopping at Mom's candy store. On our payday, Mom set up her little candy store on top of the clothes dryer in the laundry room. She took pride in displaying little wax bottles of flavored liquid sugar, wax candy lips, Tootsie Rolls, and packs of candy cigarettes. With our macaroni allowance, we could even buy full-sized candy bars. We nearly lost our minds with excitement.

On special occasions, some of our accumulated macaroni allowance could be redeemed for cash. Mom taught us how to save for something special, a valuable lesson we still practice.

One day, Dad invited Terry and me to run errands with him. It was a big deal to be asked to go to town with our father. When Dad was done, Terry and I thought we'd head home, but Dad parked in front of the corner drugstore instead. "Come on, let's get a treat," he said. We followed him to a bank of cushioned, shiny stools.

Dad motioned for us to climb up on the stools. We twirled back and forth, grinning at our reflections in the mirror across from the long marbled counter.

Dad turned to us and said, "What do you want?"

Dumbfounded at having a choice, we stopped twirling and asked him what he was getting.

He said, "My favorite, a root beer float."

Terry and I ordered the same. If Dad liked it, we'd like it too.

When the frosted mugs were placed on the counter in front of us, we learned about instant gratification. We sipped and slurped the cold root beer until we had to spoon the ice cream out of the glass.

In subsequent days, we got in trouble for arguing over who was going to do chores for Mom. We annoyed her by asking over and over what we could do to earn more macaroni. Every so often,

Terry and I asked for some of our elbows to be converted to cash instead of candy. We were then allowed to walk the quarter of a mile to the drugstore and that glitzy soda fountain. We always ordered root beer floats.

A few months after this wonderful allowance system was put in place, all four of us had dentist appointments for cleaning and check-ups. The dentist had gone to high school with Dad and felt quite free to express his alarm at the condition of our teeth.

"What on earth has been going on, Mary?" he asked my mother.

She blushed, and without going into detail, admitted, "I guess I've been more lenient in allowing them to eat sweets."

And that, as I remember, was the end of Mom's macaroni allowance candy store but the lessons we learned about earning, saving, and dental hygiene are still with each of us today.

Chicken Soup for the Soul - Best Mom Ever!
101 Stories of Gratitude, Love and Wisdom
Published 2017

9

Don't Drink the Poison

It had been a busy morning at the Health Services Center where I worked as the nursing supervisor, when I got a life-changing phone call. A disembodied voice said, "Mrs. Panko, your son has been in a fight, and you need to come to the principal's office to get him."

I prayed as I raced to the parking lot, got in my car, and drove the eight blocks to the high school.

Finding my way to the principal's office, I encountered my son sitting in a straight chair, being verbally pummeled with questions from an agitated man whom I assumed was the principal. Something was off. The man seemed oblivious to Tim's disorientation.

Even without my nursing assessment skills, I could tell he was hurt. He was bruised about his head and face. Both eyes were bloodshot, and his pupils were unequal. Alarm bells went off in my head. While the overbearing principal droned on about the rules about fighting in school, I asked Tim to tell me how many fingers I was holding up. He couldn't get it right and was confused about the day, date, and time. Finally, I held up my hand to the annoying man in charge. "Quiet! He's hurt. I'm taking him to see a doctor, and I'm calling the police."

"The police? Why?" The man was clueless.

"He has been assaulted. Can't you see that? Where is the kid or kids who did this?"

"Uh, they must have left school. We can't find them." He said sheepishly.

I led my son from the room. Tim just kept asking over and over, "Mom, did I eat lunch?" I felt like I was going to throw up.

Arriving at the offices of the medical/surgical group for whom I worked, I led Tim in through the back door and was greeted by one of the nurses I knew. I quickly gave her the rundown of his condition, and she led us into a suite where Tim could be examined. Soon, the room was crowded with medical personnel, my friends and co-workers. One took Tim's blood pressure; another got oxygen on him, another performed neurological checks while conveying information to someone on the phone. He turned to me and said, "We're calling an ambulance to take him to the hospital. Tim has a concussion, maybe even a brain contusion, and we don't have a pediatric neurologist in town. Nancy, we may have to Life Flight him to the trauma center sixty miles down the road."

I looked at my friend, Olivia, and said, "Liv, get me a paper bag." I sagged to the floor while holding onto my son's limp hand. Tim was in and out of consciousness even though we continued to get him to "stay with us." Liv handed me the bag into which I breathed in and out, trying to slow my rapid breathing.

The ambulance delivered Tim to the hospital, and my husband, George, met us there. The next thing we knew, our only son was lifting off in a helicopter from the hospital landing pad and flown to the trauma center. We had to drive while the chopper was in the air. The only comfort we had was that Tim was accompanied by a trauma doctor and nurse.

When we arrived at the hospital and found Tim's cubicle in the ER, we couldn't believe our eyes. He was alert and sitting up eating a popsicle!

The doctor at his side explained, "His neurological signs are much better. He definitely has a brain contusion, but there's no bleeding. He has some amnesia, which may or may not clear up. You can take him home, but he's got to rest with absolutely no exertion for a few days."

We gently hugged Tim from both sides to Tim. "Thank God!"

"Can you tell us what happened, honey?"

He told us a story of a guy who saw his girlfriend talking to Tim at lunch. the boyfriend became so enraged that he and his friends ambushed Tim outside the cafeteria, pummeling his head until he was semi-conscious. Finding him bleeding and crumpled in the hall, a friend took him to the nurse's office. Tim knew his assailant. That name became embedded in my consciousness as the embodiment of evil.

Tim recovered except for some amnesia. However, I began having headaches and nightmares about this faceless young man beating my son. I'd wake up in a cold sweat.

Two years later, while working at the health services center on campus, I grabbed the sign-in sheet to attend to the next student. I froze—it was the name emblazoned on my brain, the kid who had assaulted my son and got off with only a year probation. I put down the clipboard and turned to another nurse, telling her, "Donna, please take care of this one. I just can't." I went to the lounge and sat with my head in my hands, shaking.

Donna came to get me when the young man had left the building.

"He's here at the university. I can't believe he came to the infirmary," I said.

Donna replied, "Maybe he didn't know you worked in Health Services."

At our staff meeting the next morning, I asked all my co-workers for solutions to this situation. My friend Anne offered, "Maybe he won't come again." She thought a minute and offered some wise words. "Nancy, you've lived with this agony for two years. It's as if you have taken poison and expected *him* to die. The only solution is to forgive him for what he did to Tim. It would be giving a gift to yourself."

I thought about Anne's words for weeks. It finally hit me during Lent. Could I give up my hatred toward someone for an evil act against my family? It was time.

I had been asked to speak at one of the fraternities on campus one evening. During my talk, I choked on my own saliva. I signaled for someone to get me a drink. A young man jumped up before anyone else had a chance to move, ran out of the room, and came back with a bottle of cold water. Our eyes met. It was *him*. I said, "Thank you."

He said, "You're welcome."

Something in me softened.

The next day, I sat down with pen in hand and wrote a note to the young man telling him I was giving a gift to myself—a gift of forgiveness to someone who had hurt my family. It was not to excuse or condone the act. It was simply to say, "I forgive you." Putting a stamp on the note, I sent it out. I felt like a huge weight had been lifted off my heart. I was done drinking the poison.

Chicken Soup for the Soul - The Best Advice I Ever Heard
101 Stories of Epiphanies and Wise Words
Published 2018

10

Together Again

At the age of ninety-one, my Dad had fought the good fight, but no longer had the will for the daily battle. Hospice was called in to make his final days comfortable.

My sister, Judy, and I met with the end-of-life professionals in the Rehab center. After the initial assessment, the nurse was straightforward in telling us, "Your father is actively dying. It could be a few days, but no longer than a week."

With this information, Judy and I were at Dad's bedside every day. Neither of us wanted him to be alone when he died.

Two days before he died, I entered his room. I noticed how pale and still he was. I leaned close to whisper in his ear. "Hi Dad, it's Nance, I'm here." There was no response. I wondered if he was in a coma. I laid my head on the pillow next to his and began to say the Lord's Prayer. "Our Father who art in Heaven…,"

Dad began making sounds in the exact cadence as my words. He was praying with me! I realized I had been given a gift. A week prior, Dad professed his faith in God to me after decades of considering himself faithless. It was a turning point for him. Our quietly devout mother had died twelve months earlier. Since then, the only thing Dad talked about was wanting to be with Mom. They had been inseparable during their seventy-one years of marriage. Selfishly, I wanted and needed to have a sign that Dad had made it to Mom's side when he passed on.

I drew a chair next to his bed and sat quietly holding his hand. Our time together was coming to an end. I stayed later than usual that day, reluctant to go home. I was sure the nurse would call during the night to tell me Dad had died, but the phone didn't ring. I slept until the alarm went off at 7 a.m.

As I dressed to leave my house for the rehab center that morning, I looked out my bedroom window. An overcast sky and generally gloomy day reflected how I was feeling, my heart was heavy. The storm clouds were building in dark, layered formations across the sky.

Arriving at the center around 9 a.m., I walked the familiar long hallway to Dad's room, greeting staff and residents along the way.

I paused in the doorway, Judy was already there, sitting next to the bed, holding Dad's hand. Dim light from the only window in the room was diminishing, as the dark storm clouds enveloped the building.

I hugged Judy and asked her if he was responsive. She shook her head: no. The sky outside the window had taken on a deep purple hue, a prelude to a frightening, but spectacular show. In minutes, an intense wind began to howl and driving rain pelted the window. Cloud-to-ground lightning flashed repeatedly throughout the afternoon.

Dad's breathing slowed. My daughter, Margie, and granddaughter, Emily, arrived. Three generations of women counted the seconds between breaths. A sense of peacefulness enveloped each of us as Margie read the twenty-third Psalm aloud. It had comforted Dad days earlier.

The end was near. Each of us dabbed at the tears trickling down our cheeks. We watched as Dad's facial features relaxed.

There was a startling crack of thunder, followed by a flash of lightning. We all flinched, but Dad remained still.

Suddenly, his eyebrows raised as if he saw something pleasing.

A low rumble of thunder shook the windows in the care center. Our legs could feel the vibrations in the floor of the darkened room. The lights in the building flickered.

One corner of Dad's mouth curled upwards as Margie read, *"Yea, though I walk through the valley of the shadow of death, I will fear no evil ..."*

With that, Dad exhaled for the final time.

The storm outside began to subside. Beams of the late afternoon sun sliced through a section of the dark clouds, paring away a core for a staircase of light that touched the ground outside Dad's window.

Speechless at the sight, I felt God had created a miracle and sent me the sign I needed. Dad and Mom were together again.

Chicken Soup for the Soul - Messages from Heaven and Other Miracles 101 Stories of Angels, Answered Prayers, and Love That Doesn't Die
Published 2019

11

No Room at the Inn

When our children were younger, and all four of my siblings lived within a twenty-mile radius, our annual Christmas tradition started on December 24th with the entire clan gathering at our parents' home in the country. As my husband and I left the bright lights of the city with our two children, the youngsters oohed and ahhed at the stars now visible in the dark sky. Margie, age thirteen, and Tim, age eight, were excited to get to their grandparent's home to begin hanging stockings.

Over and over I explained that Santa's presents under the tree were nice, but the real reason we reveled in the season is the birth of Jesus. However, it seemed that the presents they hoped Santa would bring consumed most of their thoughts.

Besides loads of homemade Christmas goodies, part of the joy of going to Grandma's was our nuclear family being able to celebrate Mass at St. Joseph the Worker Catholic Church. A tiny, picturesque white steepled wooden building, it nestled between the rolling hills of two small towns on a country road about four miles from Mom and Dad's home. The little church seated eighty to one hundred people if they all squished together. I always thought it was the perfect subject for a Thomas Kinkade painting.

We found the recently plowed parking lot full. Our car was one of many vehicles parked on the side of the road. We could see the lighted manger scene with two live sheep munching on grains while tethered to spikes secured in the snow-covered ground. While the kids ran ahead to view the creche, my husband and I approached the people gathered on the sidewalk. Someone said,

"All the seats are taken inside, and some are standing behind the last pews. I think we'll be listening to Mass over the PA system."

The words were no sooner out of his mouth when a microphone came alive, and the presiding priest announced, "Due to fire code regulations people crowded into the vestibule will have to leave the building." Several families reluctantly joined the rest of us on the sidewalk.

It was a clear, cold, crisp winter night. I looked at the crowd around me and thought, "What a wonderful turnout for this little country church, it's too bad we can't be inside."

Bright headlights from an oncoming vehicle illuminated the crowd awaiting the first hymn signaling the beginning of the Christmas Eve service. The car parked in front of the church garage/storage area across the street. A priest stepped out of the driver's door, looked at us, and said, "Merry Christmas, I'm Father Dan. I understand there's a full house. Come help me set up for Mass."

We watched as he opened one of the overhead garage doors and flicked on the lights. Beckoning to those adults in the crowd, "Many hands make light work. The chairs are stacked over there, perhaps we could get a chain going. Is anyone here an altar server?"

A hand went up, and the volunteer was given tasks to help the priest set up a make-shift altar. Searching through a see-through plastic storage box, the priest found linens to use during the service. After producing a chalice, a carafe of wine, and a bowl containing the Eucharist, Father Dan was almost ready.

The chair brigade was busy setting up rows of seating and people were filing into each row. A strong baritone voice began singing "Silent Night" and one by one everyone joined in as the preparation for Mass continued. A lady of the parish found some candles complete with drip protectors and asked the children to distribute them. When the first hymn ended, strains of "Away in a Manger" began.

Two 100 Watt light bulbs lit the interior of the unheated two-car garage as it was converted into a sanctuary. Warmth emanated from the number of bodies packed into a reasonably small space. A feeling of kinship fostered by the communal preparation for a unique Christmas Eve service warmed our hearts. Father Dan turned off the lights as candles were lit, transforming the stark garage into a place of worship.

The sermon was short with the celebrant equating our improvisation that evening to the plight of Mary and Joseph having to find shelter in a barn where their baby boy was born. He couldn't have been more impactful when he echoed what each person in the garage was feeling, but did my kids understand how incredible an experience this was?

Just then, eight-year-old Tim leaned over to me and whispered, "Mom, there was no room for us in the Church tonight, just like there was no room in the inn for Joseph and Mary. They found space in a barn where Jesus was born, and we had Mass in a garage. This was neat! I'll always remember it!" Tears of gratitude formed in my eyes as my son expressed the exact feeling I was thinking.

Chicken Soup for the Soul - It's Beginning to Look a Lot Like Christmas 101 Tales of Holiday Love & Wonder
Published 2019

12

St. Gerard and Me

In the first trimester of my fifth pregnancy, I noticed spotting. My heart sank, and I started to cry. Having experienced three miscarriages in the previous two years, I thought, "Oh, dear Lord, not again.

This pregnancy had a unique and special component because we were in the midst of the adoption process. Only weeks from getting our baby, I had the nursery ready for a little brother or sister for our four-year-old daughter. My pregnancy had put that process on hold.

To complicate matters, the spotting started as we were getting ready to leave town for what was supposed to be a relaxing vacation.

I was beside myself. Would I lose this baby I was carrying? Would we lose the baby we'd been waiting almost a year for? Would we lose one and then the other?

The obstetrician saw me that day, and after the examination, patted my hand, encouraging us not to change our vacation plans. "You've been through this before. You know what to do, if the bleeding gets worse, get to a hospital."

Sobbing on the way home, I completely dissolved into a blob of worry and despair with the thought of possibly losing both our babies. George did his best to calm me down even though he shared my thoughts. He made me realize that I had to find my "zen" to give the baby inside my body the best chance to survive. We finished packing for our vacation and left that afternoon.

George managed to say all the right things on the long drive, and while he drove, I prayed for God's blessings for us and both our unborn babies.

Our rental was from Saturday to Saturday. Our regular routine was to unpack, drive to Alexandria Bay, go to early Mass, and then get groceries in town before heading back to the cottage.

Mass at St. Cyril's was crowded on a summer Saturday night. Our favorite priest, Father Meehan was the officiant with what he called a Sixty-Second-Soul-Saver-Homily. At the conclusion of Mass, he made an announcement that I'd never heard before in all the summers we'd been going there. Father called all expectant mothers to the front of the church to receive a special religious medal. I was last in line. The church was almost empty as Father Meehan approached me. He reached out with the medal he'd been giving all the other women. Having his undivided attention, I was moved to tell this kind priest my story. He listened in empathy, held up his hand, and said, "Wait right here, my dear, I have a special medal for you."

Scurrying into the adjoining Chapel, he returned to place a beautiful silver pendant in the palm of my hand. "This is a St. Gerard's medal. He's the patron saint of pregnant women, carry it with you and ask him to intercede for you and both your babies." Laying his hands on my head he prayed a blessing as tears rolled down my cheeks.

We left St. Cyril's feeling as if we had experienced something divine.

The days of our vacation on the beautiful St. Lawrence were filled with joy, laughter, and relaxation.

Unlike the three previous pregnancies, the spotting stopped.

That Monday, I called the doctor to make an appointment. Two days later, I was on the exam table having a doppler stethoscope run over my belly when we heard a normal fetal heartbeat! Tears of joy coursed down my face and ran into my ears. This was a good start, six months to go.

Our baby through adoption was born and was given to another couple at the top of the list. We mourned this loss but knew it was the way God had intended. We were joyful that the baby in my womb continued to grow.

When I went into labor on April third, the angels were singing. With a silver St. Gerard's medal pinned to my hospital gown, I delivered a healthy baby boy.

We were taken off the list at the adoption agency. We had a "millionaire's family" that is, a girl and a boy but I continued to carry the St. Gerard's medal in my purse.

St. Gerard was not done with his intercessions. Lending the medal to other expectant mothers in distress was something I felt compelled to do. One day, a young woman came to talk to me at the university health center where I was the nurse supervisor. She was in tears because her obstetrician discovered several abnormalities in her prenatal lab work. The doctor told her the baby would have life-threatening birth defects and advised termination of her pregnancy. She and her husband were disturbed at the thought. At their request, the doctor repeated the tests with the same distressing results.

After hearing her story, I pulled the St. Gerard's medal out of my purse and told her my experience. "You're welcome to carry this as long as you need it."

She took the medal and tucked it in her pocket. Checking in with me a few days later after our meeting, I got a phone call. My friend and her husband decided to continue with the pregnancy and trust in the mercy of God. Several months later, she called me from her hospital bed. She'd delivered a perfectly normal baby girl! The doctors were mystified!

There was no mystery about it to us. We knew it was the multitude of prayers and the intercession of St. Gerard.

Chicken Soup For the Soul - Believe in Miracles
101 Stories of Hope, Answered Prayers and Divine Intervention
Published 2020

13

How to Upstage a Bride

As I was leaving the dance floor, the bride's uncle grabbed my hand and said, "You can't quit now. May I have this next dance?"

I laughed and responded in jest, "I'll dance with you right after I have this heart attack."

It was a hot evening at the nature preserve in the middle of the Nevada desert. I'd been jumping and twirling to the music with the Bride and her mother, my good friend, for at least twenty minutes. Unusually short of breath, I chalked it up to not being able to acclimate to the altitude. I needed to take a break and have a drink of water.

Fifteen minutes later, I was on a stretcher in the back of an ambulance.

After taking a quick medical history, the Paramedic knew I was a nurse and held up the ECG strip pointing to the abnormal configuration on the paper rolling off his portable machine. "Would you like to see what your heart attack looks like?"

Turning my head toward him, I could see, it was real. I inhaled the cool oxygen flowing through the tubes in my nose, closed my eyes, and gave in to overwhelming fatigue.

I remembered stepping off the dance floor desperately needing to sit, rest, and have some water. Feeling pressure on my chest, I became acutely aware that this was more than dance fatigue. I turned to my husband and said, "I don't feel well—it's my heart, please find somebody with aspirin."

The music continued as a circle of revelers gathered around the Bride on the dance floor.

George was back in seconds with aspirin tablets in his hand. *That was Miracle #1.* I took them down with one gulp of water. He had a look of concern on his face.

Suddenly, I heard a calm voice next to me. "Hi, I'm Steve." He pulled up a chair. "I'm an ER physician and a friend of the groom. Can you tell me what's happening?" *Miracle #2.*

I told him my symptoms and that I'd just taken aspirin. He nodded while monitoring my pulse. Steve said, "Your rate and rhythm are really irregular. You need to go to the ER."

My weak protestations were no sooner out of my mouth when unrelenting sharp pain radiated through my chest into my back between my shoulder blades.

"You're right—I'll go. The pain is worse and radiating."

"Good, 'cause we've already called the ambulance, and I see the lights coming."

The DJ called the Bride and Groom to cut their cake.

With impeccable timing the rig pulled up to the patio, lights flashing and siren blaring. I watched paramedics run toward me with a gurney, dodging an obstacle course of tulle adorned reception tables, and all eyes were turned toward me.

After I was loaded into the back of the ambulance, my pain intensified. I was scared I was going to die. My mouth felt like I had tried to swallow one of those tulle table cloths. I was too exhausted to talk but not too tired to pray.

We left the party in the ambulance, complete with lights and sirens. George rode upfront with the driver. The rig pulled into the ambulance bay at a Heart and Vascular Hospital, a mere ten-minute ride from the reception. *Miracle #3.* After being unloaded and wheeled into the waiting area, My nurse brain was alert enough to notice the ER was surprisingly quiet for a Saturday night. *Miracle #4.*

Things began to happen in an urgent methodical fashion. I was hooked up to machines measuring all vital functions. Technicians came to draw blood and get a chest x-ray.

The nurse informed me how lucky I was that evening. "We have a great ER doctor on tonight, the best cardiology group is on call, and the doctor is gorgeous." *Miracle #5.* She grinned and winked. "I'll be right back with your meds."

I closed my eyes and thought, "I like her." In a minute, my new friend entered the cubicle with a hand full of syringes. "I have to give you an anti-coagulant, morphine, and something for your nausea. You'll sleep, which is exactly what your heart needs right now."

My last conscious thought was that I never got to dance with the groom.

Eight hours later, I awoke to see my husband asleep, sitting in a straight, hard chair. The pillow behind his head was resting against the wall. Someone was saying, "We're transferring you to ICU."

Upon arrival in Intensive Care, a perky young nurse announced she was taking me to a procedure room for a heart catheterization. "Maybe they'll find rice in my underwear," I pondered through the brain fog.

During the procedure, the doctor noticed I was in congestive heart failure. He immediately began treatment to remove the excess fluid from my lungs. At this point, I didn't care that I missed seeing the cutting of the cake or the tossing of the bouquet.

When the doctor arrived in the waiting area to talk to George, he said "Good news, no coronary artery blockages and no heart muscle damage." *Miracle #6.* "I think what happened last night was a series of events triggering the attack and subsequent congestive heart failure. The exertion from dancing was the tipping point. Taking aspirin was the smartest thing she did. A few days in ICU and further testing will tell us more. We'll be able to manage her on oral medication, and she should follow up with a cardiologist once you are back home in North Carolina."

I was told George sagged with relief. It certainly had been an eventful twenty-four hours. Although we missed some of the wedding photo-ops, we can probably claim that I made the most dramatic guest departure—ever.

Chicken Soup for the Soul - Believe in Miracles
101 Stories of Hope, Answered Prayers and Divine Intervention
Published 2020

14

Stuck in the Ceiling

The annoying intermittent chirps began at 4 a.m. I awoke on the second shrill beep and saw the smoke detector's red blinking light on the ceiling over my head. Half asleep, we shuffled to the guest room to catch a few more hours of shut-eye.

Over breakfast, my husband, George, announced he was going to change the battery himself. "I'm cheap. I'm not paying someone to do a job that I can do. It'll be easy peasy."

"Easy peasy my foot, George. That smoke detector is eighteen feet above our bedroom floor. You'll break your neck if you fall."

"I got this," he said smugly.

At 10 a.m., against my better judgment, I steadied a twelve-foot ladder as George stood on the top rung. He threw his left leg over the ornate crown molding of the tray ceiling and crawled onto the narrow deck. Standing up, he stretched as far as possible to reach the still-chirping smoke detector. This certainly was not a place I wanted my seventy-five-year-old husband, but, in no time at all, George had removed the dead battery and installed the new one. I sighed in relief; now, he could come down.

Kneeling on the fuzzy bathroom rug I'd tossed up to him, George attempted to get one leg over the bulky trim to reach the first step. He missed. I directed him to move left, then right, but nothing worked. After several attempts, my red-faced, husband lay prone on the deck of the tray ceiling with one arm dramatically draped over the crown molding.

I couldn't hide my concern, "Now what?"

"Go get the guys working on the neighbor's gutters and have them bring their extension ladder."

"George, they're being paid to clean out his gutters, and I don't speak their language." I walked out of the room with a feeling of panic rising in my chest.

At that point, I had no choice but to call our local fire department. I explained our "emergency."

As soon as I hung up the phone, our daughter, Margie called to check on us. When I explained that her dad was stuck in the tray ceiling, she said, "I'll be right there."

I returned to the bedroom to inform George that I'd called the fire department and was going outside to wait for them.

"Really?" He said plaintively, lifting his wet head from his forearm, "You really called the fire department?"

"Yes, I did," I said on my way out of the room. "I'll be in the garage waiting for them to get here."

Ten minutes later, Margie pulled into the driveway and hopped out of her car, running toward me. "Where's Dad?"

"In the bedroom right where I left him, stuck in the tray ceiling. Why don't you go keep him company until the firemen get here."

Five minutes later, a white pickup truck turned into our driveway. I thought, "Oh good, a fireman is here."

The truck door opened, and Margie's pastor jumped out.

"Pastor Nate, what are you doing here?"

"Margie called me. She said something about George being stuck somewhere."

"Yes, he is. Follow me, we could use a prayer right now."

I returned to watch for the firemen and was rewarded with the sight of a massive, red fire rescue vehicle parking in front of my home.

"I understand you have a situation," one of three firemen said.

"You could say that." I looked at their name tags, "Brandon, Jonathan, and Marty, my husband is stuck the tray ceiling." They tried not to grin.

"Follow me," I instructed.

The bedroom was officially crowded as six pairs of eyes looked up at my duly embarrassed husband peering over the edge of the crown molding.

Marty addressed George. "Hello sir, do you think if I guide your left foot to the top rung, you can swing your other leg over to stand on the ladder?"

"Yes, I can," George responded. "You guys didn't really need to come."

"We were in the neighborhood," Jonathan lied.

Marty said, "Sir, put your leg over the edge, and I'm going to grab your ankle and guide your foot to the ladder. Are you okay with that?"

"Yes," George confirmed. A shaky leg appeared over the top of the molding as George scooted closer to the edge. The rescue began.

When both feet were firmly on the floor, George shook hands with each fireman.

Jonathan turned to him and said, "You don't need to change batteries anymore."

George said, "Why is that?"

Brandon chimed in, "We do it free of charge."

George nodded, "Free is good."

Chicken Soup for the Soul - Laughter is the Best Medicine
101 Feel Good Stories
Published 2020

15

Slips of the Tongue

The telephone rang. "Good morning, Dad. What's new?"

"Oh, hi, Margie. Nothing much. Your mother is doing some online shopping. I think she's ordering a shroud."

"A shroud?"

"Yeah, do you want to talk to her?"

Having overheard George's end of the conversation, I snorted. I took the phone from his hand but couldn't talk because I was laughing.

"Mom, are you crying?"

"No, laughing," I managed to croak.

"You ordered a shroud?" Her voice had risen an octave.

"No, I ordered a bathing suit cover-up."

Margie began to laugh hysterically. "I hope you're writing these 'Georgisms' down."

"I am. I bought a notebook. I swear, since he retired they've gotten more frequent. I think it's because he's not having as many interactions with other people. They are getting funnier, though."

"By the way, we love the Amazon Echo you bought us for Christmas, but Dad has a hard time remembering how to activate it. One day I heard him in the kitchen, "Melissa, Alissa, Melinda …" I came into the room and saw how agitated he was. He was almost ready to throw the device."

He turned to me and growled, "This is infuriating! I am so vivid!

"Vivid?"

"Yeah, I've never been so mad at a-a-a thing."

"Her name is Alexa," I said.

He gave me a sheepish look.

Margie laughed again, "You two sure do keep me entertained."

We got off the phone, and I sat down to document the latest incident. I started reading through my collection of George's crazy mixed-up words to find they were just as funny as when I first heard them.

One day he came into the house, shut the front door, and sagged against it. I walked around the corner from the kitchen to ask if he was alright. He held his hand up, "Don't talk to me right now—I just need ten minutes to decompose."

I walked back into the kitchen, hoping his decomposing didn't make a mess in the recently cleaned foyer.

Our daughter introduced us to the delightful taste of quesadillas. We both love them, but George can not for the life of him, remember what they're called. One day he turned to me after breakfast, "Can we have conquistadors for supper tonight?"

"Conquistadors?" I had no idea what he was talking about.

"What are they?" I asked.

"You know, Margie made them for us. They're those things in a tortilla that are browned and crunchy on the outside with good meat and cheese inside."

"Ah, I think you mean quesadillas."

"Yeah, those."

"Maybe tomorrow we can have those cornucopias in the freezer," he suggested.

"I'm not sure what you mean," I replied.

I pulled out the freezer drawer and saw what I thought he was talking about, "You mean the spanakopita?"

"Yep," he confirmed. "I just love them."

"Sure, no problem." I scrambled toward my notebook to enter two in a row.

After dinner one night, we gathered all the waste cans in the house to empty them. George tied up the big white bag and, with a wave of his arm, announced, "Madame, I shall depose this garbage." He was out the door in a flash.

I pictured him as a legal eagle, recorder on the table, taking testimony from the offending bag.

He did learn to master Alexa, but requesting specific music was an occasional challenge.

From the laundry room, I could hear an argument between my husband and an electronic voice. "What seems to be the trouble?" I asked.

"I was trying to play one of my favorite country groups, Little Big Horn. It's not working," he declared, pointing to the flashing hockey puck.

"Maybe, if you asked her to play Little Big Town you'd get somewhere."

"Oh." He scowled at me.

I walked toward the desk and my notebook.

Paging through my notes, I came upon the funniest one of all times; however George was not the offender. His best friend was, but George was a willing accomplice, hanging on every word.

We were visiting our friends Anne and Bill for a few days. Anne prepared a sumptuous breakfast and went into the kitchen to retrieve cinnamon buns from the oven. Friends for over thirty years, the two men at the end of the table began to exchange stories of health issues plaguing men over a certain age. Bill related his experience of having a prostate biopsy. He reassured George, "It didn't hurt because the doctor numbed me, and it only took a few minutes. I never had any side effects, and now, all we have to do is wait for the autopsy report."

I had just taken a big mouthful of orange juice. My eyes widened, and I bolted from the table into the kitchen, and burst through the swinging door. Anne looked up at me as she held a pan of hot buns in her oven mitts. I tried not to choke as I shook with laughter and attempted to swallow.

"What did he say now?" Anne inquired. She knew her husband.

I told her. We convulsed into spasms of laughter as we leaned against the countertops. "Bill's been like this ever since he retired."

Just as I suspected, retirement is the culprit. I rest my case.

Chicken Soup for the Soul - Age is Just a Number
101 Stories of Humor & Wisdom for Life After 60
Published 2020

16

The Legacy of Mom's Christmas Stocking

As a small child, I remember hanging stockings over the fireplace on Christmas eve. It did not bother me that they looked like my Dad's work socks.

However, using my Dad's socks bothered my mother. She taught herself to knit for the sole purpose of providing each of us with a beautiful Christmas stocking. For months we saw our pretty, forty-something, redheaded mother bent over a sheet of instructions as she created that first sock. By early December, Mom had knit seven stockings. We were thrilled to have our name embroidered across the top of a red, green, and creme-colored work of art.

I was the first to marry, and my husband was the first in-law to receive a stocking. In spite of a marriage certificate and a wedding ring, we joked that he wasn't officially a member of the family until his name was embroidered on one of Mom's creations.

With each marriage and grandchild, Mom created a new Christmas sock. By that time, she only needed to refer to the instruction sheet every so often. Each stocking was a ticket to the happiest, most chaotic celebration in our growing family.

Mom even made a couple of extra stockings, tucking them away for the next in-law or grandchild to join the family. From time to time, we'd have guests for Christmas. Usually from another country, they had no place to go for the holiday, so we invited them to join in our celebration. Mom printed their name on a plain piece of paper, and pinned it on a spare stocking. Santa made sure our guest had a sock filled to the top with oranges, walnuts, gum, socks, paperback books, and other goodies.

Sadly, we learned that stockings could be taken out of circulation. They were not exempt from estrangement, divorce, and/or death.

Our beloved brother's stocking was sadly retired after he was killed in a tragic accident.

The family was delighted in 1996 when three new babies were born, and a splashy wedding brought in a new granddaughter-in-law. Mom's red hair was turning white, her freckles were fading, and her arthritic fingers slowly worked the yarn. The soft rhythmic clicking of metal knitting needles was music to our ears. Mom demonstrated her love with every knit and purl.

When Mom passed away after a short illness, none of her daughters had learned to knit the stocking. We put her bag of knitting supplies in a storage box along with a small spiral-bound notebook in which she had written the names of everyone for whom she had created a stocking. Through the years, she crafted forty unique works of art.

Two years ago, one of Mom's youngest granddaughters became pregnant with her first child. The text messages flying back and forth among discussed who could knit a stocking for the new baby. The messages were shared with each of our daughters.

My pretty, red-haired, freckle-faced niece, Angie, called me to ask if I had directions to make Grandma's Christmas Stocking. Soon, Angie began creating the first sock, knitting as she poured over the instructions just as her grandmother had.

When the new baby arrived, one of his first gifts was a personalized Christmas stocking. It had been created using his great-grandmother's pattern by another pretty, forty-something, redhead carrying on the decades-old legacy.

Chicken Soup for the Soul - Christmas is in the Air
101 Stories about the Most Wonderful Time of the Year
Published 2020

17

Fleece Navidad

Both my husband and I are hooked on a current TV series set in the western state of Montana. Christmas 2020 was approaching, and when I saw an ad for stylish jackets, shirts, and fleece clothing all emblazoned with the logo from the show, I was positive that George would love something from that collection. I picked out a pullover fleece in an attractive, dark olive color with the golden logo on the left upper chest. The corresponding picture was classy. He's a classy guy, so I was sure he'd love it. I impulsively ordered the item without my customary investigation.

Finding a gift for my husband is a frustrating challenge every single Christmas. This seemed almost too easy.

A month passed, and I hadn't received any shipping notification. I began to worry. I didn't know what part of the world it was coming from. Would it get here in time?

A few weeks later, I received a puffy plastic envelope. Behind closed doors, I tore open the package. Some furry thing vaguely resembling a matted, dirty puppy sprang from the pouch and hung from my hands. I held it out in front of me and gasped in horror. I recognized the logo of the TV show. This was the long-awaited surprise for George. Only I was the one with my mouth gaping open. The pullover was not like any fleece either of us owned or wanted to own. "Oh, dear Lord, this has to go back," I groaned. "I knew this was too good to be true."

I notified the seller that I was returning the item, printed the return label, and packaged it up. I handed the bundle to George, who was going to the post office, telling him I was returning something that didn't meet my expectations.

When George came home from running his errands, he tossed the package on the counter and informed me that it was going to cost thirty dollars to send it back.

"Thirty dollars? That's outrageous!" I stood there with my hands on my hips, wondering what to do next.

"What is it anyway?" George edged a little closer.

"It's your Christmas present," I admitted.

"How do you know I won't like it?"

"Trust me," I said with visions of a matted dog.

"Let me see."

I tossed him the package and watched as he tore it open.

I was flustered. "It's supposed to be a fleece, only it doesn't look anything like the picture. If you don't like it, we can donate it to the thrift store."

George examined the garment. "I'm gonna try it on." He disappeared around the corner. In minutes, he reappeared wearing the fuzzy green shirt. "It's comfortable—and warm. I'll wear it around the house."

He walked into the great room and sat in front of the TV. I chuckled when I saw him wearing something I pictured on one of the late-night comedians in a silly skit.

Days followed when, after dinner, George disappeared into the bedroom and emerged wearing flannel pants, his bedroom slippers, and his furry green shirt.

Finally, one day, after he took it off. I scooped it up and headed to the laundry room. I washed it on delicate, absolutely positive that it would disintegrate. It did not. When the process was complete, I threw it in the dryer, convinced it would fit my granddaughter's Ken doll when I took it out. That didn't happen either, but when I shook the shirt out, I laughed. The pullover was even fluffier and reminded me of the shag carpet we used to have in one of our bedrooms.

I laid the fleece on my husband's side of the bed so he could put it away. Arriving home after working out at the gym, George headed for the bedroom and came out wearing his flannel pants and the shaggy pullover. I knew then that it would never be going to the thrift store.

This indestructible, imitation of a fleece turned out to be the Christmas present hit of 2020 for the man who has everything.

Chicken Soup for the Soul - The Blessings of Christmas
101 Tales of Holiday Joy, Kindness and Gratitude
Published 2021

18

I Woke Up!

My eighteen-year old-grandson, Andrew, fidgeted as he sat on an uncomfortable exam table. A straightforward surgeon announced that the lump and testicle he removed a week earlier was cancerous. I watched my daughter's face crumble, tears streaming down her cheeks. The doctor was still talking.

"It occurs most frequently in young men between the ages of eighteen to thirty — usually painless."

I had to keep myself together for my daughter and Andrew. I swallowed my own shock and fear. As a retired pediatric nurse, I listened intently while my daughter, Margie, had stopped comprehending. Although I slowly digested his every word, I was terrified about what lay ahead. Andrew was my first grandchild. When he was born, I was in the delivery room, one of the first to hold him and kiss his little forehead.

The surgeon said his office would set up the initial oncology appointment. "We'll do a CAT scan and draw some blood before you leave to determine the staging of this cancer." The doctor stood and opened the exam room door. "I'll see you again tomorrow to go over the tests. Hang in there, Andrew."

While walking down the hall, Andrew turned to his mother. I heard him say, "Thank God, I had pain. It got me to the doctor faster." These were the first words he uttered after hearing the diagnosis. At the time, we didn't realize that his attitude would set an example for the entire family.

Andrew's testicular cancer had metastasized. We prayed. Everyone we knew prayed. One day before dinner, Andrew bowed his head and gave thanks for the outpouring of support. His attitude was infectious.

When he had a port put into his upper chest, Andrew pointed out, "Grandma, this means fewer vein sticks, and you know how I hate those!" He managed to find the positive.

Chemo began. His body hurt, and his hair started to come out in clumps. His mother shaved the remainder. As Andrew joked and laughed with his nurses, he became a favorite on the unit. Each day, after six to eight hours of chemo, he thanked every caregiver.

When cancer proved to be more tenacious and aggressive, Andrew reassured all of us. "Don't worry, we'll get 'em in the next round."

Andrew was drained of stamina and perpetually fatigued. He began to have severe reactions to the chemo, causing the nurses to spring into action with other drugs to combat that particular reaction. After each incident, he rewarded the team with a weak smile and a thumbs up. He spoke slowly, "I'm glad you guys know what you're doing!"

Nine weeks later, Andrew completed his last infusion. With the battery of blood tests and scans in a folder, his oncologist took my grandson's case before the tumor board.

In a few days, we had an appointment with a surgeon who explained a recently developed radical surgery to give Andrew a better chance of long-term survival. With many risks in mind, the difficult decision was made to proceed, and the surgery was scheduled. Andrew was unusually quiet on the car ride home.

A week later, after a six-hour operation, the doctor came to update us. Several family members huddled with the surgeon outside the crowded waiting room. While we hung on his every word, a team from the operating room, dressed in green scrubs, wheeled Andrew past us on their way to the Intensive Care Unit.

Andrew was awake. Our eyes met, and he saw his entire family in the hallway with the doctor. He flashed us a broad smile and held up both thumbs. As they passed by, we all heard him say, "I woke up! I'm still here!"

Chicken Soup for the Soul - Tough Times Won't Last But Tough People Do 101 Stories about Overcoming Life's Challenges Published 2021

19

Perfect Timing

My manuscript was finally done, but two nights later, I had a vivid dream of feverishly working on it once again to make a November publishing date. I heard a gentle voice say, "Get up and write this down."

I opened one eye. It was still dark. I groaned and rolled over to go back to sleep. Then I felt someone or something lightly shake me. At first, I thought my subconscious was working overtime, but my subconscious had never done THAT before.

The voice commanded, "Get up and write this down. Do it now."

I sat up and swung my legs out of bed. I didn't hear a voice anymore. Nonetheless, I padded softly out of the room, careful not to wake my husband. Once in my office, I woke up my computer. It, too, resisted being awakened.

I recalled my dream, visualizing the changes made to a few paragraphs and additions to the text. It seemed I'd been perfecting the story for months. My fingers flew across the keyboard before I forgot what I was supposed to write. At the same time, thinking about making those edits made my stomach churn because it meant it was time to send my work to the publisher. Afraid of rejection, I was stalling, and I knew it. But, the dream seemed so real, and the voice so insistent. What was the hurry?

The story was near and dear to my heart and, at times, emotionally wrenching for me to write. Although a work of fiction,

Sheltering Angels paralleled events in my life, including my younger brother's devastating death. It took me years to work through my grief. In laying it all out on paper, I relived every heart-wrenching detail.

My writing group friends and my editor told me, "Your experience and how you dealt with it may help someone else." Intellectually, I knew that to be true.

I completed the changes shown to me in the dream. After reading it aloud, I realized that the story sounded better. The manuscript was finished. While still at the keyboard, I emailed a publisher I had used for my previous novel. Writing a professional introduction to my work, I attached the manuscript, and hit send. The book was out of my hands. Feeling a sense of relief, I went back to the bedroom where my husband was still sleeping. I showered and dressed and went to the kitchen for breakfast. Later, with a cup of coffee in hand, I returned to the computer to check my emails.

My eyes widened because I had had a reply from my publisher within one hour of sending my early morning manuscript. Never had an answer come so quickly, or at that hour. Wally, the owner of the small publishing company, acknowledged the receipt of my work and said, "Your email could not have come at a better time. I'm getting ready for a virtual meeting with all my editors about what books we will put forward in the future. Since you are an established author with us, I'm adding *Sheltering Angels* to my pile. I'll have an answer for you in a day or two."

Sheltering Angels entered into the publishing process two days later. It's debut happened on the day I dreamed. In hindsight, it's clear to me why the voice was so insistent.

Chicken Soup for the Soul - Believe in Angels
101 Inspirational Stories of Hope, Miracles and Answered Prayers
Published 2022

20

Milk Money

Early in our marriage, my husband, George and I had some tough times financially. It was hard on two meager incomes to make ends meet. When I became pregnant with our first child, my doctor recommended that I take maternity leave six weeks before my due date. At that point, budgeting became an exercise in frugality, faith, and fifty ways to meal plan with hamburger. We lived in a second and third-floor row home apartment in the city and had one car.

Each Sunday morning, George and I walked the two and a half blocks to church to save money on gas. Hand in hand, we enjoyed the serenity of the stroll.

I was enthusiastically new to my faith and was in the process of instruction in the Rites of the Catholic Church. Tithing was a concept easily grasped in terms of giving ten percent of what we earned. Earning as little as we did and needing every penny was something George and I had to reconcile. As my faith deepened and I grew spiritually, I trusted God implicitly.

One Sunday morning as we were getting ready for church, we discovered that we only had one dollar between us. Our tithe would have been ten cents. We didn't have ten cents. We didn't have two nickels to rub together. We only had one dollar bill. My husband knew we needed milk, and he wasn't going to get paid for three more days. He balked at my insistence that we tithe our last dollar.

I said. "God will provide for us. Please, George, I believe this with all my heart."

Naturally protective, my husband could only think of his responsibility to me, his pregnant wife, and our unborn child. However, he was in awe of watching my growing faith. Finally, George relented. I put our last dollar into a church envelope and tucked it into my purse before we left the house.

During our walk to church, we marveled at the beautiful fall day. The leaves had turned bright orange, yellow, and various shades of red. Releasing their tenuous hold on the trees, they fell in great numbers laying down a crunchy multi-colored carpet.

Walking back to our apartment after Mass, I had flashbacks to my childhood. My brother and I used to rake leaves into huge piles and jump into them. Once the pile scattered, we ran around kicking the leaves into the air.

As my husband and I approached our row home, I stepped off the curb into the sea of crimson, impulsively kicking my foot into the leaves, sending them into the air.

George held my hand and cautioned me to be careful. I was eight months pregnant and a little clumsy. Suddenly we saw something odd within the colorful red and orange leaves. Reaching out, George grabbed a single dollar bill from the air.

He waved the bill over his head. "Look, Nance!"

I clapped, "It's milk money! I knew God would provide. All we needed was faith."

Chicken Soup for the Soul - Believe in Angels
101 Inspirational Stories of Hope, Miracles and Answered Prayers
Published 2022

21

My January Gardenia

My mother died on April 27th after a short illness. I was wracked with grief and guilt because I missed being with her at the time of her death by fifteen minutes.

While she was still conscious, I promised her that my siblings and I would take care of Dad. I also promised her I'd be at her bedside when she passed. It turns out that I could not be in two places at one time. My Dad was only six weeks post-op from open-heart surgery and he'd been at her side for hours. He was exhausted and needed to go home. One of my sisters and I were tasked with getting Dad home and to bed. My other two sisters stayed all night at the hospital with Mom. They were with her when she took her final breaths.

As the only nurse in the family, I couldn't forget the promise I had made to Mom to be there when she died. Guilt permeated my thoughts. Looking back, I believe my grief lasted longer because of my feelings of guilt.

Nine months later, my husband was outside working in the yard on a cold, sunny January day. The doorbell rang. I answered the front door to find George standing there. "Get your fleece on and come outside. Your mother is here."

I stood there in shock. What did he mean? He beckoned. I grabbed my fleece and threw it on as I followed him down the front steps. We walked around the corner to one of my gardenia bushes at the sunny corner of the garage. In the middle of the glossy, green leaves was a perfect gardenia in full bloom. This was nothing short of a miracle because all six of my gardenias bloom only once a year—in May. I raced to the back of the house to look at the other three plants growing there. Not a hint of a bloom, just like the ones in the front—except for the single, perfect white flower.

"My mother IS here," I gasped. "She loved gardenias; she carried gardenias on her wedding day. This is a message from Mom."

George put his arm around my shoulders. "I think she's trying to tell you something. What do you think it is?" he asked gently.

"That I should stop feeling so guilty?" I said as my lip quivered.

He nodded. "You did everything you could for both your parents. It's time to let it go."

I knew he was right. There was no doubt in my mind. I stood staring at the beautiful blossom in the brilliant January sunshine. I took pictures of it to remind me of the day. Finally, I walked back into the house.

I felt lighter, as if a burden had been lifted from my heart. The gardenia blossom was a gift from Mom to me, a reminder to forgive myself and that her love for me is always in bloom.

Chicken Soup for the Soul - Grieving, Loss and Healing
101 Stories of Comfort and Moving Forward
Published 2022

22

A Purr-fect Spring Concert

The doctor said, "I think you'd be an excellent candidate for a biofeedback program."

Anxiety had infiltrated every aspect of my life, causing insomnia, a racing pulse, and stomach pain. I decided to visit my doctor, hoping he had a solution other than pills.

I eagerly replied, "How soon can I start?"

Weekly visits to a Behavior Therapist in a homey comfortable office began. For one hour, I sat in a cushy recliner with Pachelbel's Canon playing in the background. By controlling my breathing and using visualization, I learned to lower my heart rate and blood pressure. In the beginning, alarms sounded over the music if my vital signs exceeded a preset level. In time, the signals were silent as the classical music relaxed every muscle in my neck and back, allowing me to slip into a blissful, relaxed state, sometimes falling asleep.

I completed my therapy and graduated with my own recording of Pachelbel's Canon. I practiced at home, putting on a headset before my head hit the pillow. My husband reported how quickly he heard a soft snore coming from my side of the bed. If I started to feel anxious at work, I excused myself for five minutes to practice my new breathing techniques. Fellow nurses noticed that I was a more relaxed version of myself.

Weeks later, I started a new job as a staff nurse at the University Health Center. Attending many collegiate social functions, I became acquainted with most of the administrators on our small campus.

One day I opened an invitation to the President's Spring Concert. I was excited for the opportunity to attend.

The evening of the concert arrived. I carefully chose an aisle seat, in case I wanted to leave early. The administration officials started filing into the auditorium. The president entered and greeted me with a handshake. He and his wife took the seats directly in front of me. The vice-presidents followed and sat next to, and in back of me. I was surrounded by the top brass of the University. I wasn't sure an early escape would be advisable or even possible.

The conductor rapped his baton on the music stand. To my enjoyment, the orchestra began with show tunes and other well-known numbers. Scanning the program, I saw the next selection was Pachelbel's Canon in D.

I panicked. As the orchestra struck the first few notes, I pinched my leg to the point of pain. This was no time to snooze.

Strains of the familiar tune took control and, despite the pinching, I began to relax. In seconds, my chin lowered to my chest, and I nodded off.

Hearing applause startled me. I regained my composure, straightened my skirt, and prepared to enjoy the remainder of the concert fairly confident that, in the dim lighting, no one was aware that I had had a nap.

Just as I thought my faux pas had gone unnoticed, the vice-president next to me leaned over and said, "You must have enjoyed that last selection quite a bit, Nancy. I heard you purring."

Chicken Soup for the Soul - Too Funny
101 Hilarious Stories to Brighten Your Days
Published 2022

23

Good Girls Get Ice Cream

My mother's signature on all her paintings and each ceramic piece she created was a small, hand-drawn heart. After she died, my daughter Margie took a picture of Mom's little heart on one of her creations and ventured into a tattoo parlor for them to make a transfer. That day, she had the delicate heart inked on her left wrist. My niece did the same. Then my granddaughter Emily followed suit and got the symbol on her shoulder.

Margie and Emily began an insidious campaign touting tattoos while in my presence. Tats were not in my wheelhouse, never had been and never would be. Even though I'm a nurse, I'm a coward when it comes to having things done to me. I didn't get my ears pierced until after eight-year-old Margie got hers done. She sat bravely on the stool at the piercing kiosk at the mall while I looked at earrings until she was done. I couldn't even watch. When we left the shopping center, I took her for an ice-cream cone. On the next trip to the mall, my school-aged daughter held my hand as I got my ears pierced. It turned out there was nothing to it. Afterward, we went for ice cream.

Margie and Emily's campaign for me to get my heart tattoo started years ago. Certainly, it was different from my personal decision to get my ears pierced. Now, I was seventy-eight years old. Finally, I admitted that, copied from an original that my mom had drawn in her own hand, the tattoo would certainly have special meaning. Still, I resisted, and still, they persisted. One day, I weakened and said, "All right, all right, I'll get the tattoo." Margie immediately made the appointment.

Two days later, the three of us were in the car. The tattoo parlor was not at all like I had pictured. It was light, bright, clean, and welcoming. There were private rooms complete with chairs like a dentist's office.

Margie asked, "Are you nervous?"

The artist placed the transfer over my wrist. "Is this where you want it?"

"Perfect!" I replied. I turned to Margie. "No, I'm not nervous. Should I be?" I turned back to the artist and asked how long it would take.

He said, "Not even a minute."

My granddaughter held out her hand. "Here, Gramma, just squeeze my hand."

"Why will I need to squeeze your hand?"

The artist dipped a sterile needle into black ink. He started his work. I heard buzzing, but I didn't look.

My eyes widened. I reached out to squeeze Emily's hand.

The artist pronounced, "There, you're done!" He placed a sterile bandage over the top of my mother's adorable, hand-drawn heart on my right wrist. I was glad I did it—and equally glad it was over.

Margie proclaimed, "Twenty-two seconds! That's how long it took."

Emily did a little dance, singing, "Grandma's got a tat. Grandma's got a tat!"

"Okay, you two. I was a good girl. Now, take me for ice cream."

Chicken Soup for the Soul - My Wonderful Wacky Family
101 Loving Stories about Our Crazy, Quirky Families
Published 2022

24

Just Ask

I couldn't believe the offer I was reading. "Yes, I'd love to do your TV show," I typed. Months before this email conversation, I wouldn't have had the confidence to ask the question.

My convoluted journey began as I undertook a nearly impossible mission to re-create my father-in-law's military history. All of his records were gone. His medals were gone, his citations had disappeared, and, to add insult to injury, the army records center in St. Louis, Missouri, had suffered a fire destroying Dad's records. I wanted to fill in the blanks for my husband and his siblings, but Dad was no longer with us to give me information.

When Dad died, we stayed at the family home during the services. My husband, George, searched the cedar chest in his parents' bedroom for evidence of his Dad's military service, one item in particular. He returned to the kitchen with a small, tattered book so worn that one could barely read the title. Putting it in a plastic sandwich bag, he tucked it in his suit coat pocket before we left for the funeral.

George was unusually quiet, so I asked him, "What is that?"

"A prayer book Dad carried through his time in the Army during the Battle of the Bulge and the Rhine crossing, the turning point of World War II," he answered.

"Oh! Wow! It is special," I responded.

"More than you know. Dad gave it to me before I left for basic training in 1961. I carried it during my tour of duty." His eyes glistened with unshed tears.

The light dawned. "I know what you're going to do with that," I said.

George nodded, "I have to, you know."

I nodded, thinking of our only daughter getting married the same day as her grandfather's funeral.

Later, in a small evening ceremony at Fort Drum, New York, George and I watched as our daughter, Margie, and her fiancé exchanged vows two days before he was to deploy for Mogadishu, Somalia with the 10th Mountain Division. The newest member of the family would be the third in line to receive the fragile prayer book.

Meanwhile, after a full year of research, with the help of surviving veterans who served with Dad, I was able to gather all his missing Army records. With the help of our Congressman, I got Dad's medals restored. Two three-ring notebooks held the documents detailing the day Dad left for basic training until he was honorably discharged. We discovered a hero we didn't know who seldom spoke about the war. The family definitely had a keepsake. I thought my mission was completed.

When our son-in-law returned home, having survived what became known as Blackhawk Down, he returned the prayer book to us in an emotional account of how it saved his life.

The re-creation of Dad's military history now had another amazing story within it. Over fifty years, three generations of service members carried the same prayer book. From the battlefields of World War II in the 1940s to the dusty street fighting in Mogadishu, Somalia in 1993, the prayer book was in their pockets.

I held the newly returned military missal in my hands and said, "If only you could talk." It was then that I had an epiphany. Maybe I could be the voice of the pocket missal. What if the missal became an animated narrator of the story?

Eight years later, *Guiding Missal* was published. Who knew this historical fiction novel would evolve from digging into Dad's military history? Writing a book is hard work, but it's only the first step for an author. Marketing and publicity are equally difficult but necessary.

Developing my concise response to "What is your book about?" was the first step. A well-known marketing expert helped me work up a "pitch sheet." I knew I had a well-edited, unique book, but I wasn't quite sure how to sell it and myself. Prepared with business cards, pitch sheets, and a biography, I was ready. I was only lacking confidence. Learning to "toot my own horn" to promote *Guiding Missal* was a challenge. I shared with my writing group that I was reluctant to approach newspapers, magazines, TV, and radio personalities for fear of being rejected.

My wise friend, Cynthia, advised, "If you don't ask, you don't ever allow anyone to say yes. What's the worst thing they could say? 'No? Get lost?' But what if they say, 'yes?'" Others in the writing group agreed.

My son, Tim, equated my dilemma to a sports metaphor. "Mom, you'll miss 100% of the shots if you don't take them."

My daughter, Margie, wisely commented, "Mom, The answer is always 'no' if you don't ask."

I took their advice and contacted the host of a local TV show I'd met in a social setting. He loved my story and said, "yes," he wanted me on his show. Two months later, *Guiding Missal* and I were on his TV segment he called "The story of a book about a book."

I pitched a radio talk show, and he loved the idea. Since then, there have been newspaper and magazine articles, interviews, and podcasts.

How did it happen? I simply asked.

Chicken Soup for the Soul - The Advice That Changed My Life
101 Stories of Epiphanies and Wise Words
Published 2023

25
Held by an Angel

I sat by Andrew's hospital bed watching him sleep, grateful that my oldest grandson had a temporary respite from pain. I gazed at the metal cage holding multiple skeletal pins protruding from his right leg; the staff referred to it as an external fixator. He had a full-length immobilizer on his left leg, and his torso was encased in a complicated brace.

I recalled a conversation my husband and I had with Andrew only five nights before. He was excited to tell us about his new job working for a roofer and the prospect of making enough money to support himself. I couldn't help but voice my concern about being on rooftops. He assured me that they'd be training him and providing safety gear. I was still not convinced and had an ominous feeling about his new occupation.

That November 16th was already not a good one. It had been raining for days, and now the temperature had dropped. My cell phone rang. I saw Andrew's picture pop up on the screen and wondered if the wet weather had him home from his roofing job.

I put my cup of tea on the table and swiped the phone.

"Hi, Andrew."

"Andrew's fallen off the roof; he's hurt."

"Andrew, it's not nice to scare your grandma like this, so knock it off."

"Ma'am, This isn't Andrew."

"Who is this?"

"I'm Jason. I work with Andrew."

Just then, I heard a scream of pain in the background. It was unmistakably my grandson's voice. He screamed again. I asked Jason, "Oh, my gosh, that's Andrew. How bad is he hurt?"

"Bad. One leg is about six inches shorter than the other. The paramedics are here, and they're trying to get his boot off. He told me to call you."

After learning their destination was the Level 1 trauma center in town, I said, "Tell him I'll come to the hospital as soon as I get dressed."

Andrew's mother was in California on business. My husband and I were the adults he and his younger sister called if a problem arose when their mom was out of town.

I threw on some clothes, grabbed my purse, and left for the hospital.

Arriving at the trauma center, I checked in and sat anxiously in the waiting room. No one allowed me into the trauma room or even gave me any idea about Andrew's condition. I didn't know that he was having the first of three orthopedic procedures to save his right leg.

Finally, I was paged to enter through the automatic doors. I met a nurse in the hallway pushing my grandson's bed to a room. I followed along. Andrew was groggy from pain medication but managed to smile and lift his hand when he saw me.

Once settled in his room, Andrew slept as I sat by his bed. A nurse came in to check his vital signs and surgical sites. After learning that I was a retired RN, she confirmed what I had gathered from the conversation in the elevator. In addition to the multiple crush fractures in his right leg, Andrew's left leg was broken with multiple ligament injuries to the knee. He would need more leg surgery after the broken vertebrae in his back had been resolved.

As he awakened, he grimaced in pain. I squeezed his hand.

"God sure loves you," I said. "From what I've heard this morning, you fell three stories. You surely must have a guardian angel."

Andrew was silent for several minutes. "Grandma, when I was falling, I felt like someone was holding me in their arms."

He paused, "The Paramedic told me that I missed hitting the wooden deck and the cement patio by inches either way. If I had hit them, I wouldn't be here talking to you."

I blinked back tears.

He swallowed several times, "Grandma, I do have a guardian angel - she was holding me."

Chicken Soup for the Soul - Angles and the Miraculous
101 Inspirational Stories of Faith, Miracles and Answered Prayers
Published 2023

26

A Perfect 10

I shaded my eyes as I watched a towboat pull para-sailers high in the sky over the ocean. It looked so easy. I settled back in my beach chair to enjoy the warm sun and fine white sand on Lucaya Beach in the Bahamas.

I turned to my husband, George, "I would love to do that someday."

"Well, here we are," he said. "You're not going to have this chance back in Pennsylvania."

"You know I'm afraid of heights," I reminded him. "I'd have to be half drunk to try it."

Just then, a Bahamian man walked by with a cooler. "Get yins cold beer!"

George signaled him, I'll take two and come back in 15 minutes. He handed one to me and said, "Bottoms up."

We were on Spring Break in the beautiful Bahamas with our two kids, fourteen-year-old Tim and nineteen-year-old Margie. For months I looked forward to putting my toes in the sand while enjoying a good book in an exotic tropical paradise. On the other hand, I wanted something exciting as well.

"This oughta be good," Tim said as he nudged his big sister.

I chugged the beer. George handed me the next one.

Margie, a freshman in college, leaned forward and asked, "Mom, do you want a funnel?"

I wasn't quite sure what she meant, but I drank another beer. A tall, lanky Bahamian man walked up and down the beach to recruit people for a parasailing adventure.

George exuberantly waved his arms. "Over here!" he shouted while digging into his bathing suit pocket to find his "beach money."

Both kids stood up and gestured toward me. Fueled with liquid courage, I eagerly followed the man to a wooden boat powered by a small outboard motor anchored in three feet of water. The man would take me out to a large square float, beyond the breakers, about fifty yards from shore, the staging area for parasailers.

The tide was coming in, and the craft bobbed up and down. I grabbed the side of the boat in the trough of the wave cycle and pushed down with my arms while I tried to hoist my leg over the side. After several feeble attempts, the kind Bahamian man behind me said, "I gun help, plenny."

On the next trough, I felt two big hands on my backside. The wave lifted the boat, and the man raised his arms over his head catapulting me into the boat as the craft splashed down into the next trough. I landed - SPLAT - between the seats, flat on my belly like a beached whale. I could hear George's guffaws and my kids howling with laughter as the motor powered the boat toward the staging area.

We came alongside the float, where half a dozen people waited their turn. I joined them watching all the activity in a semi-detached daze. The next person was harnessed and awaiting instructions to stand on the X and get hooked up to the parachute. I realized there was only one more person ahead of me, a visibly nervous lady. We chatted briefly. I tried to reassure her but found my palms sweating despite the ocean breeze. As she soared into the sky, I heard her squeals of delight — or screams of terror. I'm really not sure which.

One of the assistants beckoned me to step up to the X and put on the harness. I did as I was told. I couldn't wait to be able to say that I parasailed.

My new friend, the one who squealed in delight, was hovering for a landing when those of us on the float heard the motor on the towboat cut out. Without power to pull her, she went straight into the ocean with the parachute drifting down over her.

I gasped and put my hands to my mouth, "Oh, no! That's not good." I started to have second thoughts about this adventure.

Just as quickly as it had stopped, the motor started up again, and the boat surged ahead filling the parachute with air, lifting her out of the water. One more go-round, and the pilot assisted my friend to stick a perfect landing.

At last, it was my turn to parasail. Before I knew it, the assistants had hooked me up to the chute, and the towboat took off. I sailed straight up into the bright blue sky, finally remembering to breathe. It was so beautiful and quiet four hundred feet up in the air. I could see all of Lucaya Beach and half of Freeport. The marina was full of gorgeous yachts. Palm trees swayed in the tropical breeze, fish swam in the water. Wait—I could see fish. That meant they were BIG fish because, by then, I was sure I was at least several miles above the earth. I saw a school of gigantic rays flapping their big wings as they glided gracefully in the water around the float I'd be returning to.

The towboat turned, my parachute lost some air and flapped, seeking to be refilled. I panicked. "I'm gonna die!" I thought. I reached up to grab above the O-ring where my harness attached to the parachute. I reasoned if my harness broke, I'd still be able to hang on because I had a death grip on the lines of the parachute itself. To comfort myself, I sang at the top of my lungs - "Jesus loves me this I know, for the Bible tells me so…" The boat turned again, and we were headed for the postage-stamp-sized float somewhere beneath me. "Oh Lord, don't let them dunk me in the water," I prayed and continued to sing, "Yessssss, Jesus loves me …"

The captain did not fail me. I landed like a feather on that postage stamp. It was truly an experience of a lifetime. I looked toward the beach where my family waited for me. I started laughing when I saw that each was holding a sign with the number 10 written in black.

Chicken Soup for the Soul - Just Say Yes
Subtitle to be determined
Published 2024

27

Guests for Christmas Break

Our daughter was beside herself. "But Mom, I have to bring Rocky and Balboa home with me. It's too cold for them to stay in this drafty sorority house for a month. We have to figure something out." We continued the discussion while loading the family car for her to come home for Christmas break. We had a two-hour drive, and it was bitterly cold.

Usually, I don't mind when Margie brings friends home to visit, but Rocky and Balboa were snakes. In her Junior and Senior years as a student at University, she attended classes, worked in her free time and diligently cared for her two pets. Her reason for snakes as pets? After years of disappearing personal items, none of the sorority sisters ever came into her room to borrow clothing or jewelry.

I hated snakes. Snakes terrified me. The thought of traveling for two hours with two boa constrictors more than three feet long each made my skin crawl.

Margie persisted in her argument. I resisted even though she presented the information that, if cold enough, the snakes would get sick and die.

She had been deprived of normal furry pets because of allergies. We introduced fish, turtles, and frogs to her as a preschooler. Fish and amphibians were still in favor, but while in Brownie Scout camp, she was the only one who hunted snakes and wasn't afraid to pick them up.

I wondered, dear Lord, where was the compromise this cold afternoon in December?

"Mom, I'll bring my whole aquarium, and they won't get out, I promise. Please, I don't want them to get sick. I'll put them both in a pillow case and hold them on my lap so they stay warm from my body heat on the way home." It was a valid plan, or so I thought.

"Okay, let's finish loading. We need to get home before it snows." I shuddered, thinking of my slimy, squirming passengers.

We left the college town in North Central Pennsylvania later than planned. Both Margie and I were hungry. We had to stop for something to eat before getting on the interstate that traversed hundreds of miles through mountains with no convenient services available.

Pulling into the parking lot of a family restaurant, I looked sideways at Margie. "What are we going to do with these guys?" I gestured toward the undulating floral pillowcase.

"Uh, we have to take them in with us."

I gasped.

She continued, "It'll be too cold in the car within minutes." She pulled the pillowcase close to her body. "I'll put them under my coat."

We got out of the car and walked into the warm storefront. After being seated, Margie lay the squirmy knotted pillow case on the bench seat beside her. We scanned the menu for something quick and tasty.

The waitress approached and took our order. She didn't notice anything out of the ordinary. Our food came, we ate, and paid the bill. As we were getting our coats on to leave, the waitress stopped by to thank us and noticed the pillowcase moving on the seat.

"Uh, what is that?" She pointed at the floral bag. Margie and I looked innocently at each other.

Margie was quick to reply. "Oh, I'm taking home some dirty laundry."

"Dirty laundry, eh? The suspicious waitress replied.

Margie nervously giggled and said, "Merry Christmas, gotta run."

We waved, took our heavy pillow case, and made a hasty retreat to the car. With the heater going full blast, I asked Margie, "How are the boys doing?"

She opened the bag to check. "Settling down, Mom. I can't believe I detected a bit of concern from you, the person who hates snakes."

By the time Margie had to return to school, my attitude about snakes had significantly changed. I learned that each of her pets had a distinct personality. I found that snakes are not slimy. I learned to bathe them when they were shedding to decrease their discomfort. I learned that, after a bath, Rocky and Balboa loved snuggling in the soft folds of my bathrobe.

One evening Margie walked into the family room to see me watching TV with a sleeping Rocky in my lap. "What's this? I thought you hated snakes."

I gazed up at her and put my finger to my lips. I whispered, "Don't wake him. Let's say I'm warming up to the idea of snakes as Christmas break guests."

I heard my daughter laugh as she left the room.

Chicken Soup for the Soul - Just Say Yes
Subtitle to be determined
Published 2024

28

Hugs From Home

I was putting a care package together for our deployed son-in-law. Between his wife, mother, sister, two aunts, and me he got a care package about every two weeks. As with most families of deployed service members, it was important for those of us at home to boost our loved one's morale as long as they were out of the country.

Placing the Pringles next to a bag of trail mix, I added two bags of beef jerky, a rolled-up Sports Illustrated, baby wipes, and a few rolls of toilet paper. I tucked in a letter that chatted about news from home and threw in a container of baby powder. For those in the desert, lip balm, gum, and hard candy are necessities. Wherever there was room, I stowed extra goodies to share with those who weren't getting care packages.

I added many prayers for his safety and hoped he could feel our love envelop him as soon as he opened the box. I taped it shut as best I could and was off to our local post office.

Finding a parking spot in front of the building was an unexpected treat that morning. As I lifted the carton, I noticed that some of the sealing tape had come loose from the center seam.

Stepping up to the window, I slid the box onto the counter. While I continued to hug the care package, I rested my forehead momentarily on top of it.

The postman looked at me quizzically. "Special package?"

"Yes. It's going to our son-in-law in Somalia and I'm sending some extra love."

Again, noticing the loose sealing tape as I released my grip, I pointed to it and said, "John, would you reinforce that for me, please."

John responded, "Sure." With that said, he wrapped his burly arms around the box, laid his head on top of it, and hugged it with all his might. "There! Sent him my love, too."

Reader's Digest published 1993

Woman's World Magazine published 2019

29

What a Difference a Day Makes

I was getting ready to go to work and was in the kitchen eating the last of my breakfast. It was a gorgeous September day in north central Pennsylvania, with clear blue skies, brilliant sunshine, and leaves at the tops of the nearby mountains just starting to turn. The television was on, and regular programming was interrupted by a news bulletin to say that at 8:46 a.m. an airplane had crashed into the North Tower of the World Trade Center in New York City. My heart skipped a beat.

The telephone rang twice in succession. I answered twice to speak to our daughter and then our son who asked the same question, "Where's Dad?"

"In New York City."

"Have you heard from him?"

My answer was the same each time. "No, but I'm going to call his assistant, Phyllis, to see if she knows his schedule today. As soon as I hear anything I'll call you."

Upon disconnecting from the kids, I placed the call. My eyes were glued to the television screen as the phone rang at Woolrich, Inc.

Riveted in front of the breaking news, I was no longer interested in breakfast or work. I watched and listened as the reporters speculated as to why a plane would or could hit such a prominent building in lower Manhattan. My husband was in the city on one of his routine business trips. Phyllis answered. I told her what happened. George' staff in Woolrich turned on their TV set in the break room. Phyllis assured me that when she reached him, she'd have him call me.

Minutes later, George was on the phone. Phyllis told him what happened. Although he was in mid-town Manhattan, news from the lower part of the city hadn't yet reached him. While we were still talking, I watched as the cameras trained on the buildings captured a second aircraft as it flew into the South Tower. All major networks covered the incident and, by this time, everyone knew it was deliberate. I cried out, "George, New York is under attack. You have to get out. Get the car, and leave NOW."

"Nance, I can't. I'm standing here in the lobby of the hotel. We're getting reports from an officer at the desk that all the bridges and tunnels are being closed. I couldn't leave if I wanted to."

"Did you check out already? Rooms are going to be scarce."

"I did, but they're assuring me a place to stay tonight."

"What are you going to do now?" I asked.

"I'm going to keep what client appointments I can, and go to the meeting we have scheduled this afternoon. I'm not sure how many people will show up under the circumstances. I've got to stay busy, or this will drive me crazy."

"If you can, call me later. I've heard on the news that all the cell towers are shut down."

"I will. Yeah, I'm lucky I can use the hotel's land line. The desk clerk tells me that they'll inform guests as soon as the NYPD has opened up an exit route. Right now, only emergency vehicles are getting into the city. I have to go so someone else can use the phone. Love you, bye."

I was relieved that he was safe, and that the hotel assured him they had a room, and he wouldn't be spending the night on the street. I guessed that being a client of thirty years has its perks. However, I had an ominous feeling that the attacks were just beginning.

I faced both the TV screen and the window looking out over the valley through which the West Branch of the Susquehanna

River flowed. It was eerily serene considering what was happening to the east of us in New York City.

Around 9:10 a.m., I saw a large passenger plane pass over our valley heading west. I thought it odd because, although we were in the flight pattern, planes were usually at a much higher altitude. I glanced back at the TV set broadcasting news bulletins from New York City and reports of aircraft all over the nation being grounded. I looked back at the plane flying over our valley getting smaller in the distance. Why was that plane not grounded? I had a strange sense of foreboding. Was I overreacting?

At 9:37 a.m., American Airlines Flight 77 crashed into the western side of the Pentagon in Washington, D.C. killing fifty-nine aboard the plane and one hundred twenty-five military and civilian personnel inside the building. Three attacks on our nation in less than an hour. We were definitely under siege. How many more people were going to die today?

The South Tower of the World Trade Center collapsed at 9:59 a.m. TV cameras caught it all. Evacuees, on-lookers, and reporters ran for their lives. People fleeing the site were covered from head to toe in grey ash. I thought of our friends who worked in those buildings. Were they safe?

The media began to report conversations heard by Air Traffic Controllers from the cockpit of one of the hijacked planes. Family members at home were talking to loved ones on the aircraft with messages of love and final goodbyes. Passengers told family members they were attempting to take back United Airlines Flight 93 in the air over Pennsylvania. In an emotional conversation with his wife, Todd Beamer uttered those famous words to his fellow heroes, "Let's roll!" In response to the resistance, the hijackers deliberately crashed the plane into a field in Shanksville, Pennsylvania at 10:07 a.m., killing all aboard. Investigators learned that Flight 93's original mission was to crash into the Capitol Building in Washington, D.C.

I couldn't stay at home alone to think about everything happening and my husband being stuck in the city, so I went to work for a few hours. The office was subdued. Patients were calling to cancel their appointment stating they were too upset to sit in a dental chair. Everyone seemed to be moving robotically, just trying to get through the day.

As soon as I got home, I emailed my friend Jay who worked at the World Trade Center. "Please contact me. I'm worried about you," I typed. I awaited word from family members of others.

After a fitful night's sleep, I answered the phone at 8 a.m. George called to say the NYPD had opened one lane of the George Washington Bridge for traffic leaving the city. He would be home in about four hours. I offered up a prayer of thanksgiving and began to plan a meal of comfort foods. We were going to need comfort.

On September 12, 2001, American flags flew from every house and business in Lock Haven, Pennsylvania. The national news showed the same phenomenon from coast to coast. The nation was united in shock, grief, and mourning. Citizens stood shoulder to shoulder with a profound sense of patriotism.

In later days, the nation got details of Firefighters, EMTs, Law Enforcement Officers, and ordinary citizens who did extraordinary things to save lives that day. The passengers who valiantly fought hijackers for control of Flight 93 were among these heroes.

Epilogue:

On September 14, our son called to say there was no news from his friend Martin who worked for Cantor Fitzgerald in the North Tower. The family hoped that he had survived, but the odds were not in his favor. The reporters began interviewing survivors and family members who spoke to their loved ones inside the burning buildings. Cantor Fitzgerald could not account for six hundred fifty-eight of their nine hundred sixty workers occupying floors 101 through 105. When American Airlines Flight 11 flew into floors 93 through 99 of the North Tower, the Boeing 767 was traveling at four hundred seventy miles per hour. The aircraft measured one hundred fifty-six feet from wingtip to wingtip and carried 10,000 gallons of jet fuel. After the initial impact, a shock wave radiated up and down the building shaking the huge structure. We prayed for a miracle that Martin would be found safe.

Three days later, I received an email from my friend, Jay. He recounted that he watched as the second plane hit the South Tower. His building was evacuated, and everyone ran for their lives as the buildings collapsed and spewed thick gray ash over all of lower Manhattan. He walked for hours, eventually crossing the George Washington Bridge on foot along with hundreds of others. Once on the Jersey side, he called for someone to pick him up and take him home. Thank God, he was spared.

Hearing that my friend Amy was safe at home after the attacks on New York City was another huge relief. Amy was eight months pregnant. She and her husband were eagerly looking forward to being first-time parents. She worked at American Express across the street from the World Trade Center in a job she loved, in the city she loved.

On the morning of 9/11, Amy was thinking about her nine a.m. meeting as she crossed over the West Side Highway via the pedestrian bridge. She was startled by a loud roaring noise and began to see white papers falling from the sky. Everyone ran, including eight-month-pregnant Amy. She made it across the bridge into the atrium and joined up with a friend. Grabbing Megan's hand tightly, Amy took charge, and led her through the streets to the water's edge a few blocks away where they could clearly see black billowing smoke pouring from the North Tower. They were told that an airplane had hit the building. At that moment, the growing crowd at the dock seeking to escape the inferno heard another low-flying jumbo jet. They watched in horror as it banked and plowed into the South Tower, spewing fuel and flames throughout the damaged floors. It was then everyone knew New York City was under attack.

Amy and Megan found seats on a crowded ferry. Amy insisted that the crew give her a life jacket. She told me that all she could think of was Pearl Harbor. She was convinced that the ferry boats would be attacked next. If she was wearing a life jacket, she reasoned, at least she would float enabling someone to save her and her unborn child.

The two young women had no idea where this ferry would dock, they just knew they had to get away from the carnage. When the boat pulled into a berth at Hoboken, it discharged hundreds of passengers and returned to the New York side to retrieve more.

The two women found their way to the New Jersey Transit, and boarded a train heading west. As they rode in silence, the women checked for cell service. As soon as they could, they called their frantic family members to meet them at the station.

Amy related to me that it was a tearful, joyous reunion but that night, she could not begin to close her eyes. The aftermath of an intense survival mode adrenaline rush had worn off and anxiety had set in. She had to turn on every light in the house to feel safe enough to sleep.

One month later Amy delivered a healthy baby boy. It was almost a year before she returned to work in the city. Everything had changed. Not one employee could sit on the side of the office to look out the windows facing east. Where the once majestic World Trade Center Towers stood was a deep, dark pit in the earth. Many people in the office found themselves breaking into tears from the mere proximity of what remained as a result of evil perpetrated upon our nation that glorious fall day in September. Workers still combed through the debris looking for evidence of those unaccounted for.

One day, I got a call from my son that, like a needle in the proverbial haystack, Martin's wedding ring had been found in the rubble. His wife identified it from the inscription inside. Martin's family finally had closure.

After reading the National Transportation Safety Board report some years later, my husband and I determined that Flight 93 had been the aircraft I saw flying above the West Branch of the Susquehanna. It was not my imagination. This nation had gone from living in freedom one day, to living in fear the next. The United States of America was forever changed.

9/11 That Beautiful, Broken Day
Published 2021

Other Favorites

30

About Your Canoe...

A carpet of thick seaweed trapped several dead fish in its green tentacles. A strong current had pushed the junk into the L-shaped corner between our boathouse dock and the adjacent dock along the retaining wall. The seaweed stunk to high heaven. Floating pieces of tree limbs got caught up in the mass as the winter ice melted. Dad said we had to get it out of our cove. My husband and brothers-in-law were tasked with the job.

Bill got into Dad's antique flat-back wooden canoe with an old three and a half horsepower motor mounted on the stern. It was Dad's pride and joy, and ran like a charm. While Bill had the bowline around a cleat on the dock, he revved the little motor.

The rest of us used rakes to push the seaweed out of the corner into the whirlpool created by the prop that was supposed to shove the green mass into the main river. Dad went back into his workshop. For some reason, the wind or the current was against us. Bill had the brilliant idea to release the bowline and to steer the canoe into circles creating a larger whirlpool. Bill's turns became tighter because the handle on the motor was up against the gunwale. Eventually, the canoe rolled over with Bill in it.

Jeff, George, and I watched the upside-down boat sink into the seaweed soup. The propeller continued to turn in the air until completely submerged.

Water temperatures in the St. Lawrence River at that time of the year hovered around fifty-five degrees. The depth in that spot was seven to eight feet. Jeff, George, and I stood on the boathouse dock to watch and wait for Bill to surface.

Jeff pronounced, "That water's cold, I'm not going in."

I echoed, "I'm not going in either. He'll come up."

George started to pace, "Maybe someone should go in."

Jeff looked at his watch. "Bill is a strong swimmer. Let's give him a minute."

The time had just about expired when we saw a mound of seaweed rise above the surface of the water. As the mound grew, it moved toward the dock. Then we saw an arm protrude through the seaweed, it was holding the bowline of the canoe. Bill was under all that seaweed! He had managed to hang onto the rope even as the boat capsized.

Despite having a wet, limp cigarette dangling from his mouth, he hollered, "I saved the canoe!" We burst out laughing at the sight of our seaweed monster.

George and Jeff were able to help Bill get out of the water in between bouts of laughter. Jeff grabbed the bowline, and all three hefted the submerged canoe out of the water and onto the dock. We sagged onto the retaining wall to catch our breath. The sun was warm, and the bizarre incident was over. Rehashing the event from each of our perspectives caused more laughter to echo across the bay.

Sobering up, I said, "Dad was in his workshop when all this drama happened. I don't even want to be around when he hears the story."

"Okay, guys," Jeff said. "Who's going to tell Dad what happened to his prized canoe and motor?"

"Yeah," a voice said from behind us. "Who's gonna tell Dad?"

Our eyes widened and one by one we turned around to see Dad dabbing at the tears streaming down his cheeks, bent over in laughter. It seemed he knew …

"At least the seaweed is gone," Bill choked out, "But, um, Dad, About your canoe…"

31

The Money Shot

Wanting to update my Facebook photo, I scrolled through my pictures. One of the first to appear was over forty years old, the image of a student nurse. A flood of memories consumed me, and my eyes threatened to leak. I clicked on the picture and made it a part of my profile.

I remembered the day when a letter from the Director of Nursing appeared in all our mailboxes at the nurses' residence. It said that the school of nursing was launching an advertising campaign. Professional photographers were looking at our application pictures for a suitable candidate to be the "Angel of Mercy" representing Williamsport Hospital School of Nursing. I shrugged and ran off to class.

A week later, I received another letter saying I was one of three chosen for a professional photo session. I laughed out loud at the crazy turn of events. I was the oldest nursing student in my class in fact, I was the oldest student in the entire school. I was thirty-six, and before this endeavor, it had been seventeen years since my last college experience. Why on earth would they choose me? I commuted fifty-two miles a day. When could I possibly fit in a photoshoot?

My husband and two children were priorities that I had temporarily realigned to pursue this career. I recalled the family meeting during which we discussed the venture. If there had been one "no" vote, it was over. My husband, George, was my biggest supporter. Our daughter, Margie, was twelve when I began classes at our local university; our son, Tim, was six and a half. Each of them opted to take on more household chores during my schooling. They urged me to "go for it."

The letter said, "We will work around your schedule." Well, all right then. We quickly agreed on a date and time for my session.

I dressed in a clean student nurse uniform and my prized cap. As freshman, our class had not even had our first striping ceremony; my cap was pure white, devoid of any black velvet stripes designating one's level of education and experience.

When I arrived at the temporary photography studio set up, bright lights with umbrella-like structures were positioned around a bench seat in front of a plain background. The pros directed me how to sit, turn, look up, look down and give them a Mona Lisa smile. In the darkness, I heard a voice say, "Look toward Heaven —and moisten your lips."

I swallowed the lump forming in my throat and prayed that my chin wouldn't start to quiver. *Why did he say Heaven?* I looked up and thought of my younger brother, killed in a tragic accident four years earlier. He was the impetus for my return to school, fulfilling a life-long dream of becoming a nurse. His death spurred me to make something of my life beyond being a wife and mother. I thought about my brother while everything else faded away. I heard a different voice from the darkness whisper, "There's your money shot." I was aware of several clicks of a lens. And then, "We're done. Thank you for your time. The Director of Nursing will make the announcement soon."

I got up from my seat, grabbed my backpack, and headed to my car in a daze. The experience had been somewhat surreal but spiritual. I felt like I'd had a connection—a moment—with my brother. Whatever it was, it was a gift. I brushed a tear from my cheek and pulled myself together for the drive home.

A couple of days later, I received the announcement that my picture had been chosen as the nursing school "Angel of Mercy" to run in prime time television commercials for six weeks.

I managed to see the final product twice during my intense class schedule, once after The Dukes of Hazard and again during Saturday Night Live. While my kids were thrilled at my newfound celebrity status, I concentrated on making the Dean's List.

In my senior year, during our Intensive Care rotation, I was assigned a nineteen-year-old patient whose condition shook me to the core and sent me to my knees in prayer. "Lord, give me strength and send angels to help," I begged.

Sam was injured in the same way as my late brother, but my brother had died instantly. Sam was on life support after having two brain surgeries, not expected to live. I was solely responsible for his care on the 7 - 3 shift. Although Comatose, two weeks later, Sam began responding to commands. He struggled to regain consciousness. One day, he began breathing on his own and I was able to remove the breathing tube and take him off the ventilator. It was a miracle in which I felt blessed to be a participant. As soon as he was well enough, Sam was moved to a step-down unit and then to Rehab.

After completing my ICU rotation, my former instructor told me that Sam's mother took her aside to ask if I was actually a student nurse because she believed I was an angel sent by God to help her son.

After twenty-five years of nursing, I retired. Serious health issues came unexpectedly. In my recuperation, I began to write.

Forty years after my six-week reign as the "Angel of Mercy" for the nursing school, my second novel, *Sheltering Angels* was published. Based on personal experiences, the story of a little girl born with the ability to see and talk to her guardian angel hit the market in the midst of a pandemic. *Sheltering Angels* was awarded second place in its category in a talk radio book contest. Six months after that honor, the book won a silver medal for literary fiction.

Little did I know when I went to change my Facebook profile picture that I would have a remarkable journey down memory lane to revisit so many incidents of divine intervention.

32

The Pink Ninja

Dressed in my favorite fuzzy pink bathrobe with matching slippers, I emerged from the bathroom with a toothbrush stuck in the corner of my mouth. As I shuffled down the hallway to the guest bedroom, I heard my name mentioned. My nephew, Greg, was trying unsuccessfully to get his eight-year-old son to settle down for the night and must have heard me in the hall.

I stopped in my tracks to listen.

"Aunt Nancy's a Pink Ninja, Tyler. Did you know that? Maybe she'll tell you a little about her adventures before you go to sleep."

I turned to see Greg's eyes plead for help.

I stuffed the toothbrush into my flowered cosmetic bag and set it down. Tyler's room was dimly lit, but I could see the blond-haired boy in Buzz Lightyear pajamas with matching sheets pulled up to his chin. Tyler had his arms behind his head and gazed at me expectantly.

"Aunt Nancy, are you REALLY a Pink Ninja?" His blue eyes narrowed.

Greg slithered past me as he conceded the bedtime routine.

I sat on the edge of Tyler's bed, took a deep breath, and whispered, "Can I trust you?"

"Yes," Tyler whispered back.

"You can't tell anyone what I'm about to tell you. Promise?"

"I promise, Aunt Nancy."

"Your dad is right. I AM a Pink Ninja."

He gasped. "Have you fought the forces of evil, Aunt Nancy?"

"I have." I tried my best to keep a straight face.

Rather than getting sleepy, Tyler was energized by our conversation. He sat up and started gesturing with his arms.

"Aunt Nancy, did you use the Ninja weapons?"

Good grief, I thought, where was I going with this story? I didn't have the vaguest notion of what was in a ninja's bag of tricks. How was I going to fake this one?

I need not have worried.

"Aunt Nancy, did you use the throwing stars?"

I nodded enthusiastically and gave him a thumbs-up.

"The nun-chucks?"

I nodded again and gave him a high five.

"Can you rappel off the side of a building?"

"You bet I can! That's one of the first exercises ninjas learn in basic training. You gotta know that one to escape after a mission."

"Did you go on many missions, Aunt Nancy?"

"Too many to count. Here's a secret: One of the basic rules in ninja training is to get eight hours of sleep before a mission. Now, how 'bout you lie back and close your eyes. I will answer all your questions in the morning. I promise I'll still be here."

"Okay. G'nite, Pink Ninja."

"G'nite, Tyler."

In the morning, I sat at the counter drinking hot coffee as Tyler danced around with question after question. I found it entertaining to think fast. I sipped while conjuring up secret missions against deadly evil forces. When Tyler became animated, I was a more inspired storyteller.

The charade continued for several years, even though I suspect Tyler was on to me. It was just too much fun for both of us to stop.

As a teenager, Tyler showed deference to his aging Aunt Nancy. Even the younger nephews were keen on finding out why. I suspect Tyler shared what he knew.

One day, at another family gathering, five-year-old Mason sat down beside me as I was watching television. He leaned into me and said, "Are you really The Pink Ninja?"

I replied in surprise. "Who told you that, Mason?"

"Tyler says you are the Pink Ninja, for real."

"Do you believe him?"

"Yep," he said, nodding vigorously.

"Well, I'm retired now, but I have to confess - I was a Pink Ninja, Mason."

Mason crossed his arms and snuggled closer, "I bet you still got it, Aunt Nancy."

My four nephews are now in their teens and early twenties and still refer to me as Aunt Nancy the Ninja. Apparently, my life as a ninja had an impact on them.

33

What a Hoot!

Our friend, Chuck, called to us across the hotel lobby, "Meet us at Hooters for lunch - at 12:30. It's right across the street."

My husband and I gave him an affirmative thumbs up as the elevator door closed. I turned to George, "I'll call Anne to let her know; maybe she'd like to join us."

We were in Charlotte, North Carolina—retired charter members of a prestigious credit group that George and Bill, Anne's husband, started decades ago. This gathering gave us a chance to reconnect with old friends and kick up our heels, so to speak.

At 12:30, we entered the Hooters restaurant. George and I saw Chuck waving to us from a booth in the back of the room. As soon as we were seated, a Hooters girl greeted us. After introducing herself, she enthusiastically explained the lunch specials and took our drink orders.

When the beverages arrived, Chuck addressed our server. We should have known by the twinkle in his eye that mischief would ensue with Chuck's unrivaled comedic timing. He said, "You know, miss, you are in the presence of greatness. Do you see the colors my companion is wearing?"

The server's blue eyes widened as she looked me up and down. Chuck had noticed, but I was unaware I had worn Hooters colors, orange and white with black accents. Neither commented that I was wearing a lot more fabric than she was.

Pointing at me, Chuck said, "She was an original Hooters girl!"

George choked on the water he was drinking.

"Really?" The young lady said.

"Yes, indeed. When the first Hooters opened in Clearwater, Florida on October 4, 1983, Nancy was wearing the very uniform you have on now."

I thought the girl would faint. "Wait till I tell the others." She turned toward the clutch of fellow servers gathered at the end of the bar.

"Wait, there's more." Chuck looked past the waitress to see our friend Anne walking toward the booth. He started to laugh but quickly gathered himself and spoke authoritatively. "We are joined today by yet another original Hooters girl who opened up that Clearwater establishment."

George's face was beet red from trying to stifle his laughter. My eyes met Anne's as she slid into the booth giving her a signal to "Play along."

Our server looked directly at Anne and gasped. "You were there too?"

Anne responded, "I guess I was."

Pointing across the table at me and then Anne, "And that's why you two wore Hooters colors today. Oh, this is awesome."

Ironically, Anne had also dressed in orange and white with accents of black. "Yes, that's exactly why." Anne quietly affirmed.

Chuck slapped the table top and announced, lifting his glass, "Ladies, in honor of this auspicious occasion, lunch is on me. Let's toast to the pioneers known as Hooter girls!" Despite my career as a nurse and Anne's as a Dean at a well-known university, we owned up to the fable of starting out as Hooter girls.

Without calculating the math, from the 1983 launch of Hooters and our apparent ages to validate or repudiate our claim, the server gleefully clapped her hands, and ran off to share the news with her coworkers.

Chuck wiped the tears streaming down his face and said, "I was reading the history of Hooters on the back of the menu and saw Nancy in those colors and just had to do it. When Anne walked in wearing the same colors, it was too rich. I just had to take the story home. Forgive me, ladies."

The old Hooters girls were laughing too hard to care. Chuck was paying for lunch.

34

A Note for the Teacher

Anyone who has ever had a puppy, especially a black lab, knows they are a chewing machine, at least for the first two years. Doctor Pepper was no exception. At three months old, he ate the bottom of my broom until he was up to the wire wrapping and could go no farther. Doc ate my Dad's sandals, and the plastic handles on the kids' saucer sleds. He shredded one pair of our son's sneakers. In addition, the dog could climb like a champ. So, it was no surprise when I had to write a note to a teacher excusing my dog's behavior.

After wolfing down his breakfast, our black lab puppy was sleeping in his kennel in the garage.

Tim and his best friend Chris walked to the bus stop every day. One day, Tim was running a little late. When the boys were ready to leave, they had to run two blocks to make the bus. They bolted out of the kitchen door into the garage. Doctor Pepper was curled in a ball nestled into his blanket when he was awakened by the ruckus the boys made as they approached.

The sleepy puppy raised his fuzzy head, and Tim reached through the open kennel door to scratch his pet behind the ears. He noticed that the pup had white flakes covering his thick coat.

"What have you been doing?" He asked. Doc responded by shamefully laying his head on both paws and looked at Tim with soulful brown eyes.

Meanwhile, Chris screamed, "My notebook, my homework!"

"What are you talking about?" Tim turned to Chris and noticed that he held the remnants of a spiral notebook. The only things left were the metal spiral and some shreds of paper.

"Oh no!" Tim said.

Chris lamented, "Doc ate every page of my homework. I'm gonna get an 'F.'"

I was finishing the breakfast dishes when I heard the commotion in the garage. I walked through the kitchen door, and heard the last of Chris's comments.

"Doc ate your homework? How did that happen? How exactly did OUR dog get YOUR homework?"

"I left my notebook on top of his kennel."

"Well, that explains it. This crazy dog climbed on top of the kennel."

"But, I never thought he could get my homework." Chris moaned.

"Boys, come back into the house. Chris, I'll write you a note, and then drive you guys to school."

Tim stifled a laugh. Chris failed to see the humor in the situation until both boys followed me into the kitchen and heard me verbally composing the note.

"Dear Mrs. Smith, I am not making this up. This really happened. Our climbing commando puppy ate Chris's homework. I have a feeling you may want to call me. Sincerely, Nancy Panko (Tim's mother)" 555-666-1234

35

A Lasting Impression

My husband. George and I decided to shop at the Company Store one Saturday morning. Our two-year-old son, Timmy, played quietly at my feet beneath the round clothing rack. The store was crowded with sale shoppers, and I was concerned that he would trip or scare someone, so I bent down to pick him up.

George approached me from the men's department with a distinguished-looking older couple. At the same time, Timmy screamed in protest because he did not want to be removed from his hiding place. After I extracted him from a tangle of garments, our normally docile toddler turned into a red-faced banshee. I was shocked.

Not to be deterred, George began formal introductions to the couple. I heard snippets, "on the Board of Directors." (for the company for which my husband had just been hired) I also heard, "This is Marguerite and John..." and "The founder's grandson."

I thought, "These folks are bonafide VIPs."

As George talked, our crazed baby arched his back and lurched forward to grab my ears. Screaming at the top of his lungs, he pulled my ears as far from my head as the cartilage would allow and then head-butted me. Timmy was not done exacting revenge because he lunged forward again and latched onto my nose with his little teeth. The older couple looked on with slack-jawed disbelief at what was happening before them.

I moved away from my wide-eyed husband and the VIPs, skirting the clothing racks and the growing crowd of sale shoppers, toward the exit. I managed to get through the doors to the parking lot while my demon child was still clamped onto my nose and trying to rip my ears off.

As soon as we were outside, I popped his diapered bottom to make Timmy stop biting my nose. Exhausted, I sagged to the curb with my normally docile son in my lap.

We both sat in the parking lot crying, and that is where my husband found us. He pulled a handkerchief out of his back pocket and dabbed at the blood on my nose. I winced and moaned, "I'm so embarrassed at the spectacle that happened in front of all those people. I'll never be able to show my face in this store again, much less to face John or Marguerite."

George gathered us in his arms and reassured me that everything was alright, despite Timmy's behavior leaving a lasting impression on my nose. "Marguerite said to tell you that she has been in that very same spot with each of her four kids, and they grew up to be fine, responsible adults."

36

Stormin' Norman and Me

In 2005, my husband and I attended the 175th-anniversary celebration of his employer, Woolrich, Inc. The company hosted a day of family fun for all employees in the town park. The company, founded in 1830, achieved some notability from producing woolen blankets for the Union Army during the civil war and its tradition red and black checked hunting clothing. Hundreds of employees, from the president to the janitors, were eating hot dogs, participating in horseshoes and corn hole, posing for pictures with clowns, and dancing to live music. A famous guest speaker drew television crews from nearby cities to cover the event.

    Sometime after 12 Noon, we saw three black SUVs with dark-tinted windows pull into the park and travel on the back service road. The CEO walked over to greet the dignitary—our keynote speaker. Retired General Norman Schwarzkopf, affectionately called "Stormin' Norman," alighted from the vehicle and was immediately surrounded by five bodyguards in fatigues.

    Norman Schwarzkopf was a Vietnam War veteran, commander of the U.S. Central Command, and a four-star general in the U.S. Army. In 1991, Schwarzkopf led Operation Desert Storm, the U.S. military effort to liberate Kuwait, driving out Saddam Hussein's forces in only six weeks.

    I remember following every news report on TV, in newspapers, and in magazines on General Schwarzkopf. I always wanted to thank the man for protecting our country and for the impressive job he and his forces did.

After his inspirational address, he agreed to have pictures taken with the employees of every department. General Schwarzkopf took time to shake hands with each person. I was even more in awe of the man. My husband's department was last on the schedule. The process was moving along on time until storm clouds gathered.

Thunder rumbled, and lightning lit up the sky. When the rain began, my husband and I were among two dozen people who sought shelter under a large canopy set up for refreshments.

The sounds and lights of the storm made me jumpy, but so did having a national hero behind me under the canvas. General Norman Schwarzkopf stood at least 6'5" and was as wide as a door. His five bodyguards were even more imposing.

Here was my chance to talk to this national hero. In a tent. During a thunderstorm. I started rehearsing my words. "Thank you for your service" seemed trite. "I respect you, and thank you for your patriotism." Maybe. My heart was pounding. I tried to take slow deep breaths to calm down.

George glanced at me and said, "Are you all right?"

"Yeah, I'm trying to get up the nerve to approach one of those big guys over there to ask if I can shake the General's hand."

George's long-time assistant leaned into me and said, "Go for it. The storm is starting to pass. If you don't do it now, you'll lose your chance."

I took another breath and walked toward the general. Two of his bodyguards stepped in between "Stormin' Norman" and me. I am only 5'1" and I found it strangely amusing that they viewed me as a potential threat.

To the taller one, I said, "May I shake the General's hand."

He nodded and stepped aside.

I moved forward and extended my arm. This famous general, a bear of a man, took my small hand in his giant paw and firmly shook it. His face softened, and I saw a hint of a smile.

All of my rehearsed words immediately left my brain. I croaked, "Thank you" and burst into tears.

He nodded. Embarrassed, I scuttled back to my husband who comforted me. "Don't worry, he knows how you feel. He's talked to both grateful and grieving families many times. He knows." I sniffled and blew my nose.

The rain stopped, and the sun emerged. After the general shook hands with the remaining employees, "Stormin' Norman" posed for the last picture of the day.

The impassive retired general stood at attention but, like the sun, his kindness shone through.

37

Are Slips of the Tongue Contagious?

I had just started a load of wash when I heard my husband George shouting at the television on the other side of the house.

"That was a fragrant foul! Come on Ref, call it!" He shouted.

"What's happening?" I inquired as I walked into the great room.

"This game is too close for lousy calls from the referee," he responded. "You have to be blind to miss those fragrant fouls."

"Yeah," I responded. "That just stinks."

My husband is the king of malapropisms in our household. I write them in a notebook because they keep the family entertained. Some days he showers me with several of his unique terms.

One evening I was preparing dinner. George looked over my shoulder, and announced that he wanted mariner sauce on his chicken.

"Aye aye, captain," I replied as I reached for the marinara sauce in the refrigerator."

He gave me a snappy salute and walked away to turn on the evening news. I reached for my notebook.

We regularly watch the singing competition shows on television. George has paid close attention to each judge's comments regarding song choices. One night a singer chose a number to perform out of their genre. "Wow," he said, "that number was out of her jondray."

I giggled and got out my pen and notebook.

One day, I came home after running errands to find George groaning about politics. "Congress wants to use resurrection to avoid the threat of a filibuster."

"Resurrection?" I queried.

"I know. Can you believe it?"

"Well, don't say it too loud, it'll wake the dead. Then they might vote for the use of Reconciliation," I said with a straight face.

George scratched his head at my response, and I scribbled in my notebook.

Packing a snack bag for an early morning fishing trip, George searched the pantry for appropriate items.

"Are you going to make sandwiches?" I asked while washing dishes.

"No, we need quick snacks. I'm grabbing a handful of power balls."

"What?" I turned to look at him, "Are you playing the lottery?"

He scowled at me. "Don't be silly. We can't eat lottery tickets. I'm taking these." He held up a bunch of protein power bars.

It's a good thing the notebook was already on the kitchen counter. I dried my hands and began to write.

One day, we were pleased to have our only daughter and granddaughter come to visit. Our teenage granddaughter wore a flannel shirt partially unbuttoned and off her shoulder. I couldn't help but notice the amount of skin showing. As any grandmother would do, I swallowed hard before I commented.

"Aren't you cold? After all, it's December."

"No, Grandma, I want to show off my decoupage."

"Your decoupage?"

"Yeah, my pretty butterfly tattoo on my chest."

Her mother and I exchanged glances.

She looked at me—and then her at mother with a puzzled expression. "What?"

I spoke up, "Honey, the word you want is décolletage, showing off your shoulders, but don't feel bad about the word mixup. If your grandfather was home, he'd tell you not to show so much of your decoupage which is an art form."

My granddaughter scratched her head as my daughter and I burst out laughing. I reached for my notebook.

38

Just Fourteen Days

Coronavirus came to our land and reared its ugly head.
"Follow our rules, just fourteen days," is what the government said.

Close the parks, the gyms, and pools,
Stay fit and healthy? Don't be fools.

Don't wear a mask, there aren't enough.
Stay six feet apart, things are gonna get rough.

Stay at home, close the schools.
Work remotely - don't be fools.

Just do what we say, this virus to dread,
Just fourteen days to stem the spread.

Oops, new rule: wear a mask, not one but two.
Add a plexiglass shield, you'll look so cool.

Wash your hands, and sanitize.
Do not get it in your eyes!

One shot, two shots,
me and you shots.

You need a booster, just one or two more,
to keep that virus from your door.

Mask up, mask down.
What's this? I see that frown!

COVID-19, strains of Delta, and the "Cron"
Cover your face, keep your mask on.

We've had three shots, wore masks and all.
But, surprise! COVID can still infect y'all.

Get a test, then test some more.
Waiting in line is such a chore.

The government says don't question the science,
All that's required is your loyal compliance.

Will we ever regain the life we once had?
Work, play, school, celebrating the grad?

Trust in God, and stay faithful to Him.
Your cup runneth over when it's filled to the brim.

Mute the TV, live your life not in fear.
Treasure your friends, and hold family near.

Use common sense, and take care of yourself.
A sound mind and body are your wealth.

In all things, He must be praised.
Count your blessings, and you'll be amazed.

39

High Altitude Adventure

After days of business meetings, my husband, George, and I, along with our friend, Bill, left warm and sunny Denver, Colorado, to sightsee in Arapaho National Park. Three adventurous seniors never anticipated where the journey would ultimately take us. But, there we were—14,000 feet up—in a blizzard—on a sunny day—in August. And, I'm afraid of heights in good weather.

Early that morning, we left the city thinking we were prepared for the mountains with food and water in the car. Although Denver was 85 degrees, we dressed in short-sleeved shirts and jeans. I was the only one to grab a jacket because I'm always cold. We toured Arapaho National Park, did some hiking, and enjoyed a picnic lunch. Not ones to pass up the opportunity, we decided to drive to the top of Mount Evans on our way back to Denver. Mount Evans is the highest peak in North America to have a paved road to the summit. It is, by no means, for the faint of heart. The unlined road has no guard rails and dozens of switchbacks. There is barely room for two cars to pass. Once at the summit at 14,130 feet, we expected a magnificent view of nearby Pike's Peak and the Continental Divide through the coin-operated viewing scopes. We hoped to see some wildlife typical to the area, mountain goats and big horn sheep.

At ten thousand feet, well above the tree line, Denver was a speck in the distance, and the external temperature reading on the dashboard plunged. We saw a mini-van on the narrow road in front of us. The vehicle was parked against the steep, rocky mountain wall. A young man was outside the van, pacing back and forth. Both George and Bill watched him get back in the van. They speculated that someone in the vehicle was sick or the driver panicked at the altitude and lack of guard rails. I could relate.

We crept alongside the mini-van in our full-size sedan. I slid across the backseat to the driver's side window. George heard me gasp and saw me scramble to the right side of the car.

"I see nothing but air, George." My stomach flip-flopped, and my mind raced headlong into panic mode. *Our tires have to be perched on the edge of the pavement. One false move and we'll be airborne into the abyss, thousands of feet below.* I resorted to a childhood coping mechanism, and started humming "Jesus loves me."

Just inches away from the side of the van, Bill stopped the car. George rolled down his window and signaled the man to do the same. The visibly shaken man stated he didn't want to go any higher with his family in the car. George and Bill convinced the driver to follow us to the next switchback where he could safely make a three-point turn to go back down the mountain.

Bill slowly passed the mini-van and watched in the rearview mirror as the van began to follow. At the switchback, we paused to see him execute a three-point turn and head down the mountain.

A sign announced that we had reached 12,000 feet. Snow was falling and had started to cover the road. The higher we went, the harder it snowed. The wind howled, buffeting the car. I feared we'd be blown over the side to some undiscovered crevice below where our bodies would never be found.

Bill persevered, and we made it to the summit of Mount Evans in the August blizzard. None of us could see our hands in front of our faces. We parked the car and sat there for a few minutes before I said, "I'm not getting out. Just leave the car running and the heater on." George concurred, he wasn't getting out either. The temperature was twelve degrees.

Bill said, "Hand me your coat, will you, Nancy? I drove up here to see the vista, and I've got quarters in my pocket— I'm going to see the vista."

Bill attempted to jam his upper body bulk into my jacket. He finally gave up, and settled on putting the hood over his head. We watched him trudge off to find the super-duper binoculars into which he'd insert his quarters, but lost sight of him as soon as he stepped away from the car.

"What if he can't find his way back," I whispered.

No sooner did I have the words out of my mouth when the car door opened, and Bill plopped himself into the driver's seat. "Brrrrr, it's cold out there, and I can't see a thing!"

He took a few minutes to warm up before putting the car in gear to exit the lot. Now the highest paved road in North America, with no guard rails or markings, was slick with snow. Despite being cold, my palms were sweating. I resumed humming that old familiar tune.

Inching our way down the mountain in low gear took forever to reach an altitude where there was no snow falling. When visibility returned, each of us expressed relief. I was looking out the window at the valley below when I felt Bill brake.

"Would you look at this!" I heard him exclaim.

I glanced up to see a large herd of mountain goats and Big-Horn sheep walking down the steep, rocky walls onto the road. Some casually strolled in front of our car and disappeared over the edge of the pavement. I croaked, "A camera?"

Bill rolled down his window and looked to his right to search the console for his camera, coming up empty. "George, check the glove compartment, will you?"

While Bill's head was turned and George was searching for the camera, I shrieked as an inquisitive mountain goat thrust his entire head through Bill's open window. Bill turned and came nose to nose with a snorting animal. Looking back, I believe there was kissing involved. However romantic, both Bill and George howled in surprise. I was convulsing with laughter in the back seat. I'm not sure who was more shocked, Bill or the animal.

The goat backed away, trotted in front of the car, and bounced over the edge of the road disappearing into thin air.

We did have an excellent adventure that day. I'm so glad that I hadn't let my fear of heights spoil it.

40

Danger in the Doctor's Office

One night I was the only nurse on duty in the rural office of a medical/surgical practice. Our receptionist, Sharon, excused herself from checking out our last patient to approach me at the nurse's station.

"Nancy, I heard something when I was in the bathroom. It sounded like scraping coming from either the lab or x-ray rooms. It was kind of creepy."

"I'll check it out," I told her.

We locked the doors at 11:30 p.m. when the patient left the building. I walked as quietly as I could through the hallway listening. I stopped when I heard the strange sounds. I agreed with Sharon that the noises came from the lab or X-ray rooms. I entered each area, turned on all the lights, and the sounds stopped.

I felt the hair rising on the back of my neck. Logically, I thought the noise could be an animal, considering the building was surrounded by cow pastures. Even a tree limb brushing up against the building might cause the sounds, but my sixth sense told me it was something more ominous. Sharon had the same sense of unease. We were locked in, but it sounded like someone or something was trying to get to us.

We gathered our belongings and met at the back door, poised to engage the alarm before walking into a well-lit parking lot. Once in our cars, I followed Sharon out of the lot.

I found it hard to fall asleep that night, uneasy about the danger I felt earlier.

At 8 a.m., the phone rang. The medical office manager, Elaine, informed me that the building was broken into within an hour of us engaging the alarm. The culprits cut and sawed through the outside wall and used a box cutter to slice through the soft, protective lead lining in the wall of the X-ray room. Then, they crawled through the utility sink base cabinet.

I told her about the noises we'd heard. She agreed it was unnerving to think bad guys were trying to get into the main office while we were there. I had a chilling thought of what they might have done to Sharon and me had we still been there.

Elaine explained that the main target was the locked medication room at the nurse's station. After kicking in the door, the culprits grabbed anything perceived to have street value. However, thirty seconds after they tripped the motion sensor, the alarms went off, including at the State Police barracks a quarter of a mile down the road.

She went on to say that two men were caught by the officers on site. Already known to local police, the bad guys were hiding in the bushes holding empty pillowcases. When the officers were able to enter the building, they found a trail of medication dropped by the perps in a panic to escape.

Comparing notes the next night, Sharon and I agreed that we must have had guardian angels protecting us from danger.

41

Our International Incidents

Who takes their kids to a two-day international business meeting? Apparently, we do, because here we were at a French-language-only restaurant with our two kids and the Canadian Distributors associated with my husband's employer.

A tall mustached waiter wheeled a cart to our table to prepare a flambé dish. Our eight-year-old son, Tim, watched intently, and when the flames jumped three feet in the air, I could see his wheels turning. With his index finger to his lips, Tim frowned. Then he looked up at the waiter and said in English, "Has your mustache ever caught on fire?" George and I held our breath until the waiter started to grin, and all eight people at our table laughed. The waiter broke protocol and replied in English, "No, it hasn't - yet."

It seemed like our boy had broken the ice. Everyone relaxed, talked, and laughed a little more during dinner. After a fancy French dessert, our host, Bill, informed me that a business associate would be picking the kids and me up at the hotel the next morning at 9 a.m. While the men were working on contract negotiations, we would be sightseeing in Montreal.

After breakfast the next day, our fourteen-year-old daughter, Margie, sulked in the room as Tim watched cartoons in French. She announced, "Mom, I'll be bored if we tour museums and flower gardens." She crossed her arms and stomped into the bathroom. I sighed. This was not the time for a teenage snit.

Promptly at 9 a.m., the phone rang. Our guide, Pierre, was in the lobby, he said we'd know him by his yellow golf shirt and black pants.

"We have to leave," I said to the kids. "Pierre is here."

"I'll bet he's a boring old man," Margie huffed.

I shot her *the* look and crossed my fingers.

We got off the elevator and headed to the lobby. A tall, white-haired gentleman in a yellow golf shirt and black pants walked toward us.

Margie muttered, "See, I told ya."

He walked past us. Margie and I did a double-take when we saw a much younger, definitely more handsome man approach us. He also was wearing a yellow shirt and black pants. I thought Margie's eyes would pop out of her head, and I saw her mood lift. Pierre chatted as he led us to a car for a day of fun.

That night our hosts took us to an Italian restaurant where we gathered in a private room. I didn't have to worry about Margie being bored because she and twenty-one-year-old Pierre were talking to others about the lovely gardens we visited at the site of the 1976 Olympics earlier in the day. I couldn't help but grin.

When Tim got antsy, I suggested he and I take a walk to the restroom. We stopped by a giant built-in aquarium. In it were dozens of lobsters with their claws banded. I explained to Tim that banding was necessary to eliminate the creatures fighting each other. We returned to our private room. While awaiting our entrees, Tim asked if he could visit the lobster tank again. I nodded and told him I'd come to get him when dinner came.

Ten minutes later, our entrees were served. I excused myself to get Tim.

As I rounded the corner, I could hear Tim's voice narrating a mock battle. My jaw dropped when I saw that he had rolled up the sleeves of his white dress shirt past his elbows and had both arms immersed in the tank. With a good-sized lobster in each hand, Tim was simulating a crustacean conflict. I hung back because I could hardly stifle my laughter.

Other restaurant patrons were watching in amusement. I saw a pretty girl in a pink dress approach my son.

She began to speak—in French. Tim froze. The hands holding lobsters stilled. Even the lobsters' antennae stopped moving. Tim turned his head to look at the little girl. She spoke again. His hands opened, and the lobsters dropped. Tim pulled his dripping arms out of the tank. Shaking off the excess water, he began to unroll the sleeves of his shirt. He spied me around the corner and rushed to my side.

"She's talking to me, Mom, and I can't understand her."

"That's because she's speaking French, honey. Dinner is being served, let's go eat."

"Okay." Tim looked over his shoulder at the little girl and lifted one hand to wave.

After dinner, Mr. Bill was eager to drive us to the top of Mount Royal in his luxury sedan. He invited Tim to sit in the front passenger seat and opened the moon roof to reveal a magnificent array of stars in the dark summer sky.

At that moment I knew what kind of parents take their kids on international business trips—parents who know how special their kids are. Our kids managed to charm our hosts.

Just then, Tim reclined his seat and put both his hands behind his head.

"This is the life, Mr. Bill," Tim sighed. "I wonder what the poor people are doing?"

I could hear George's eyes rolling!

42

Picture This

My husband and two kids posed for me in front of the picturesque historic church on a hill. "Just one more, please. I have to get both the steeple and the spire in the shot." I stepped back and looked in the viewfinder of my new camera, trying to capture the church and my family in the morning light. It didn't quite fit. Just one more step back should do it. Instantly, I felt myself in mid-air, tumbling head over tail across dirt, gravel, and rocks.

I lay on a steep incline in a daze, and then searing pain hit my back and legs. I closed my eyes. "Oh, Lord, please let this be a dream." I snapped out of it when I heard my family.

"Mom!"

"Mommy!"

"Nancy! Are you all right?"

I lifted a hand to let them know I was in the land of the living, although I wasn't entirely sure about that.

I heard my husband, George, and our fourteen-year-old daughter, Margie, making their way down the forty-foot rocky incline toward me. It took them a few minutes - I had made much better time.

George got to me first. "What hurts?"

"Uh, everything," I groaned. "Where's my camera?"

"It's behind your head. The strap is still around your neck. Let's not worry about that now. Your knees are bleeding. We need to get you back to the car. Can you move?"

I lifted both arms, moved both legs and winced. "Yeah, I can move. After a tumble like that, I can't believe I'm in one piece."

At that point, both George and Margie helped me sit up. Eight-year-old Tim watched our progress from atop the hill with the church in the background.

"Ooooh," I said.

"What?" George asked. "Are you okay? Do we need to lay you back down?"

"No, I was just thinking this would be a great shot of Tim with the steeple and the blue sky overhead."

"Seriously? As it is, our whole family thinks you don't go on vacation with us because you are always behind the camera." Both he and Margie seemed a little exasperated with me. "Okay, do you think you can stand?" Practical George asked.

I nodded, and grabbed onto his hands, letting him pull me up as Margie gave me a boost from behind. I reminded them, "We have a first aid kit in the car. Don't forget I'm a nurse. I can clean myself up. Just help me navigate this steep hill." The camera swung around my neck as we moved up the rugged terrain.

"I hate to tell you this, Mom, but your brand new shorts are ripped and stained with grass and mud," Margie announced, having that particular view.

That was the straw that broke the camel's back. I started to cry. "It was the last pair of pink Bermuda shorts in my size on the rack. I'll never find another pair this late in the season. I didn't even get a picture of me wearing them."

We got to the top of the hill, and I limped to the car to dig out the first aid kit. Using antiseptic wipes, I washed blood and dirt off my legs.

My young son watched me apply antibiotic ointment and bandages to both knees. "Mom, I gotta ask you an important question."

"What's that, honey?"

"Did you get the picture?

43

The Story That Changed My Life

After twenty-five years of a rewarding pediatric nursing career, I retired. Eager to travel, my husband and I went on a cruise with friends. One evening, we found ourselves exchanging stories of life-changing events. I shared a nursing school experience of my first Intensive Care Unit (ICU) patient. Our friends said, "You must write about that. Sharing could help another family."

My only brother's accidental death led me to examine my life. I'd always wanted to become a registered nurse, and had learned firsthand that life is short, so, I went back to school at the age of thirty-five. I wanted to make the world a better place because my brother didn't get the chance.

You may recall that during my senior year ICU rotation, I was assigned a young man who had suffered skull fractures while trimming tree branches around power lines.

Through answered prayers and by the grace of God, I was able to give my patient the best care possible. Despite the death of my only brother under similar circumstances only a few years prior.

I graduated that Spring and took my board exams to become a licensed R.N. Afterward, I looked back on that ICU experience and saw how it changed my outlook, personally and professionally. I knew, eventually, I had to share the story.

During the ensuing years, I attempted to write a historical fiction novel. When the subject matter became too emotional, I stopped writing. It was just too painful to continue. The manuscript sat unfinished.

Somehow I became aware that *Chicken Soup for the Soul* was requesting stories for a 2014 book titled *Find Your Inner Strength*. After reading the prompts, I started making notes. Perhaps, a short story would be something I could complete. However, reliving my brother's accident, I cried as much as I wrote.

Despite the emotions, I finished my story, "A Journey of Healing," and submitted it. Ten months later, I received an email from D'ette Corona that my story had made the first round. I was elated. When I got the news that "A Journey of Healing" had made it through the final round, I felt some validation as a writer.

During book signings people approached me with their stories of loved ones in comas. Each said my story gave them tips to facilitate a family member to regain consciousness.

With a boost in confidence, I thought maybe I had the tools to finish my dormant manuscript. At age seventy-four, I resumed working on *Guiding Missal* and submitted it to a publisher. Much to my delight, my manuscript was accepted! *Guiding Missal* won a silver medal from a national organization six months after its release.

In the ensuing years, I've published a second novel and three children's books. I credit my success to that first story, "A Journey of Healing." In addition to helping me heal from deep-seated grief, that first story showed me I could market myself as a storyteller and a writer in a second dream career.

44

Writing a book about a book

My father-in-law died after a long illness. His funeral was scheduled for 9 a.m. on a Friday in Scranton, Pennsylvania. Unbelievably, our only daughter's wedding was at 6 p.m. that same evening in upstate New York. We were grieving Dad's loss, but this sad time was just the beginning. The next two years would be an emotional roller coaster forever changing the direction of my life.

After being notified of my father-in-law's death, my husband and I drove to his parent's home in Scranton. With his mother in a nursing home, George led me into a dark kitchen. I switched on a light, and George raced up the stairs to the bedrooms, undoubtedly on a mission. I followed him to the master bedroom and watched as he rummaged through his mother's cedar chest. "It's gotta be here. I put it here. I was the last one to have it."

I left him and went downstairs to fix a quick bite to eat before we left for Dad's viewing. George joined me a few minutes later holding a little book. After finding a sandwich bag for the book, he put it in the pocket of his navy blue blazer. We ate in silence before leaving the house.

As we drove, I pointed in the general direction of his pocket and asked, "What *is* that?"

"It's a military missal, a prayer book, that Dad carried when he served in World War II. It's for service members. When I enlisted in the Air Force, Dad wanted me to carry it."

"Why did he want you to carry it?" I asked.

"It offered him protection," he responded.

I raised my eyebrows, "Protection?"

"Yeah, he came home in one piece," George said matter-of-factly.

"Oh, yeah, He certainly did," I agreed.

Returning to the house later that evening, we fell into bed. We knew the next day, with a funeral and a wedding, would be emotionally exhausting.

Our daughter was engaged to an Army Specialist stationed at Fort Drum, New York. He was thirty-six hours from being deployed to Mogadishu, Somalia in the Horn of Africa.

After the funeral, we began our four-hour drive to Watertown, New York.

At 6 p.m., the wedding before a justice of the peace went off without a hitch. When our son-in-law left for Somalia, he had the military missal safely tucked in his pocket knowing he was the third in line to carry it.

One year later, having survived the intense Battle of Mogadishu, also known as, Blackhawk Down, our son-in-law returned the missal to us. George handed it to me for safekeeping.

Seeking inspiration, I laid the missal on my desk next to the computer as I attempted to re-create my father-in-law's military history. I had nothing to go on except a crumpled, torn bronze star citation. George couldn't help me because he said his father didn't talk about his time in the war. I was even more dejected after contacting the Army Records Center in St. Louis, Missouri, when they told me that Dad's file had been destroyed in a fire. I thumbed through the thin pages of the missal and read prayers of encouragement.

Multiple dead ends left me feeling defeated. And then—a miracle. A letter from the clerk of the 289th Cannon Company in which Dad served came to light. I called the man to explain my mission. He, in turn, forwarded me a company history and a detailed journal of every battle through the end of the war. I patted the missal and said, "I'm getting closer."

Putting together the puzzle pieces of Dad's military history took another twelve months, but I now had proof that he was a decorated war hero. With the evidence presented to our congressman, I was able to get Dad's medals.

Confident that I was done, I picked up the well-worn prayer book and cradled it in my hands, whispering, "If only you could talk!" At that moment, a new seed of passion was planted in my heart. I was not done. I knew that I had to write a book about this book.

I realized that I had to be a better writer than I was. Joining writers' groups, signing up for webinars, taking writing classes, and gratefully accepting constructive criticism was a major part of my growth. With the missal next to my keyboard, I began writing short stories submitting some to *Chicken Soup for the Soul*. At seventy-one, my first of many stories was published in a *Chicken Soup for the Soul* book.

Writing a book about a book took me eight years, including that first year of research. I was seventy-fours years old when *Guiding Missal* was published. Six months later, my book was awarded a silver medal from The Military Writers Society of America. My inspirational story of faith, family, patriotism, and miracles narrated in the voice of a spirited military missal was validated.

I fell in love with a unique little book. I'm convinced that the Word of God within the pages of the military missal directed the steps of the men who carried the prayer book while in service to their country. I'm grateful that the same words encouraged and directed my creative steps to write *Guiding Missal*.

45

Miracle on the Farm

A long time ago, my family lived on a dairy farm. My father and grandfather raised grains and harvested them. We had dairy cows, chickens, pigs, and horses. My brother, Terry, and I had farm chores designated by my dad according to our age and abilities. Our assigned task could be as simple as gathering eggs from the laying hens. We were young and getting used to being around large animals and equipment.

One day, Dad was preparing to pick up recently baled hay in the fields. He hooked up the hay wagon to one of the tractors. After he pulled the rig to the front of the barn, he parked and walked toward the house to grab his thermos.

My three-year-old brother and I were playing in the backyard. Mom sat on the porch watching us as she bounced our baby sister on her knees. It was a beautiful, sunny summer day, and all was well with the world.

Dad kissed Mom on the cheek and told her he was leaving to pick up baled hay, and that he'd see her in a couple of hours.

Back on the tractor, Dad drove slowly down the dirt driveway past the house. His favorite horse galloped to the fence line and trotted at the same pace as the tractor. Dad turned his head toward the horse and laughed. He didn't see what was happening on the house side of the tractor.

Simultaneously, Terry looked up from what he was doing to see Dad on the tractor. He got up and took off in a run as fast as his little legs would carry him. "Daddy, Daddy, I wanna go!" He hollered.

Horrified, I started to see everything moving in slow motion. Dad didn't hear Terry calling him over the noise of the tractor. Terry kept running, the tractor was moving, and Mom was screaming, "Stop, Terry, stop!"

I couldn't breathe as I watched my little brother fall and slide under the dual wheels of the hay wagon.

When Dad felt the trailer go over a bump, and heard all the screaming and crying on our side of the driveway, he knew he had run over one of his children or one of the dogs. He jammed on the brakes and jumped down from the tractor. Dad's dark skin paled when he saw Terry lying under the wagon.

Mom, Dad, and I ran to my little brother. Dad scooped Terry up in his arms and lay the sobbing boy gently in the grass. Mom wailed, "I just know both his legs are broken."

Dad slid my brother's overalls down to look at his legs. Perfect tire prints were visible across my brother's thighs, but the skin wasn't even broken. Mom calmed Terry, smoothing back his hair and wiping his dirty, tear-stained cheeks with a hankie from her apron.

Terry stopped crying and looked up at Mom and Dad. "Can I have a lollipop?"

"Yes, you can," they said in unison. As Dad was pulling Terry's overalls up, he told him, "We'll get you one and you can have it while we take you to see the doctor."

Terry said, "I get it, Daddy. I know where they are." I watched my three-year-old brother jump up and run up the porch steps into the house to get his lollipop.

Mom hitched my little sister over her shoulder and went after Terry, calling to Dad, "I guess his legs aren't broken, but I should get him before he climbs on the counter and falls."

As I got older, I played this scene over in my head, realizing what I saw was divine intervention.

As a nurse, I've wondered how does a three-year-old get run over by a thousand-pound hay wagon and not get seriously injured?

46

Grandma's Advice

As I was growing up, I remember my dear grandmother sharing her wise advice. Whenever I visited her as a child, she often said, "Always wear clean underwear." My nine-year-old eyes widened when she added, "You just never know when you'll be in an accident." That was terrifying to me. Years passed, but I never forgot what grandma said.

Decades later, I was married with two kids, a house and garden. One Saturday morning, I jumped out of bed, threw on an old pair of cut-off jeans and a stained tank top to work in the garden before it got too hot. When I finished, I called out to my husband, "I'm filthy dirty already, so I'm going for a bike ride before I get in the shower."

"OK," he responded.

I pedaled up the street and saw my twelve-year-old daughter riding her bike toward me. We waved at each other. At that, a giant beetle came buzzing at my face. I yanked the handlebars to the left to avoid the bug. The front wheel slid on loose gravel, and my body continued to fly forward, landing head first on the macadam. My arms were at my sides, and the handlebars were poking me in the belly. The lights went out momentarily until I heard screams of, "Mom, Mom!"

A neighbor, Eve, heard the commotion, and came out on her front porch to see Margie kneeling in the road beside me. Eve returned to her house to grab an ice pack and a blanket. After tending to me, she sent Margie to get her father. I had an egg-sized lump on my forehead that hurt like the devil. I found it hard to form a thought or to talk because I was woozy and had gravel in my mouth. I groaned, remembering Grandma's solemn advice.

When George arrived with our car, I protested going to the hospital, "But-but, I don't have on clean underwear." I was overruled. Eve helped George get me in the car, and we went to the Emergency Room.

Lying on a hospital gurney in a small cubicle, I thought of my grandma with her hands on her hips, shaking her head, wagging her finger, "You didn't put on clean underwear." I shared that with George. He calmly responded, "Um, honey - you don't have clean anything on. No one will notice."

The doctor entered my cubicle to examine me. "What happened to you?" He asked while he looked at my swollen left eye, bloodied head, arms and legs.

Although drowsy, I managed to answer with my eyes closed, "I fell off my bike," and added under my breath, "and I don't have clean underwear on."

The doctor continued his examination and assessment. "Wow, must have been some wreck. How's the motorcycle doing?"

George responded in surprise, "Motorcycle? Doc, she was riding her bicycle!"

"Wow, I'm impressed! All this from falling off your bicycle?" He checked my pupils and turned to my husband. "Her pupils are unequal, she definitely has a concussion, maybe a brain contusion, and this laceration took off half her eyebrow. Her arm may be broken. We'll get some X-rays and get it immobilized for the time being. I want to rule out internal injuries from the handlebars hitting her in the abdomen. We'll clean up all these cuts and scrapes, then I'm going to admit her for observation.

He turned back to me, and leaned down to whisper, "Don't worry, I won't tell a soul that you don't have on clean underwear."

47

Miracle Maneuver

It was supposed to be an easy shopping excursion. It was supposed to be an uneventful outing for our family. It wasn't supposed to involve a life and death incident.

A flyer arrived in the mail announcing a tent sale by a well-known local furniture maker. It was an opportunity to purchase special pieces for our new home at unbelievable savings. The three-day-event was in early winter 1975, in a warehouse with a cement floor. We bundled up our two-year-old son, Timmy, and his seven-year-old sister. If we were in that building for any length of time, it would get uncomfortable. Our plan was to be quick shoppers.

Upon arriving, we walked up and down the aisles scanning right and left for a great buy. George carried Timmy, but within the first fifteen minutes, our toddler wanted to get down to walk with his sister.

It wasn't unusual to see people we knew from the area, so we weren't surprised when we bumped into a man who worked with George. He and his wife were doing the same kind of browsing we were. They were quite fond of our young children as theirs were grown and out of the house. At one point, George and I were inspecting a shelf unit perfect for our living room, and the kids were talking to our friends.

Suddenly, Timmy came running toward me. His face was red, and his little arms were flailing. I asked him a question, and he couldn't talk. Then I noticed that he wasn't breathing.

"Oh my Lord, George, he isn't breathing. He's choking on something." I cried aloud, "We need a doctor or a nurse!" The blood vessels in my toddler's eyes started to burst, and his lips turned blue. I picked up my son, held him face-down over my right arm, and gave him an abdominal thrust. "George, when I tell you to, sweep two fingers through his mouth, from one cheek to the other. We have to get this thing out."

I gave a second abdominal thrust, and nothing happened. On the third thrust, George swept Timmy's mouth, and out popped a piece of hard candy that flew out of his mouth and skittered across the cement floor. Timmy took in a big ragged breath. I turned him around, held him tight, and collapsed on the nearest chair.

Timmy began to say over and over, "What happen to Timmy? What happen to Timmy?"

I murmured, "You choked on some candy, but we got it out, honey. You're going to be alright.

We hadn't noticed that a crowd had gathered from my first cry of alarm. I looked up at a sea of concerned faces and said, "He'll be fine, he's okay."

We were approached by our friend, the man with whom George worked. He began to apologize. "I gave him a piece of hard candy. It's my fault. I'm so sorry. I'm just so sorry." We assured him that all was well that ended well but that we don't give hard candy to our kids at this tender age. He and his wife nodded and asked if there was anything they could do for us. We declined and said we'd be leaving soon to go home.

George turned to me and said, "How did you know what to do?"

I answered, "You won't believe this, but just this week, a new Reader's Digest came, and I read about a new life-saving technique for choking victims. It's called the Heimlich Maneuver after the doctor who first used it."

"Thank God," he murmured. "That was some coincidence!"

"No, honey, it was a miracle—a God thing. We were able to save our son."

48

January Christmas

My brother, Terry, the only boy among four girls, was stationed on an airbase in Thailand during the Vietnam War and unable to come home for Christmas. The family was operating in the "missing man formation." No one wanted to participate in our family holiday traditions without our brother being present, and he wasn't due home until late January. Therefore, our parents announced that Christmas would be celebrated on January 25th when Terry and his wife, Laura, could be with us.

After New Year's Day, Mom began playing holiday music, especially her favorite, "I'll be home for Christmas."

Everyone took advantage of after-Christmas sales with plenty of time to finish shopping and wrapping gifts. Mom and Dad began to decorate the house. After January first, neighbors took down outside lights while my Dad hung additional white lights around the deck.

As time grew closer to our brother's arrival, Mom's activities in the kitchen increased. She baked pumpkin spice bread and several pie crusts and put them in the freezer.

Besides Terry's wife, I think no one was more excited about our brother's arrival than my father. By the end of the second week in January, Dad trudged through the snow into the woods to cut down an appropriate-sized tree and brought it down a snow-covered hill tied to a sled. After thumping it on the ground to dislodge snowflakes and sawdust, Dad carried the fragrant fir into the house and set it up.

When Mom and Dad got the phone call from Laura that Terry was in the States and on his way to the local airport, they were sneaky by not telling any of his four sisters the whole story. They wanted to surprise us.

Laura, picked him up at the airport and took him to Mom and Dad's home. Mom called each of us to come to the house so we could talk to our brother when he called during a supposed layover in Chicago. Our youngest sister— who still lived at home —was surprised when Terry walked through the back door. Shrieks of joy echoed through the house as sister after sister arrived just minutes apart.

It was a wonderful homecoming. That night, we hung twelve stockings on the mantle.

No tradition was omitted. In the early morning hours, we began with the stair picture. Seated on the steps, we gathered in family groups. Dad put his camera on a tripod, carefully lined up the shot, pushed the timer, then raced to get in the picture. The resulting image showed everyone laughing because Dad fell into his spot on the steps.

Mom and Dad gave us the sign to pile down the steps and find our stockings. Everyone sat around the room admiring treasures from a colorful hand-knit sock made by our mother.

The celebration moved to the next phase—a continental breakfast with juices, homemade sticky buns, blueberry muffins, and lots of freshly brewed coffee and tea. The main event followed —nothing short of a present-opening-marathon.

The best part of the day was not the gifts or the food, it was being together, sharing laughter, hugs, and love. Everyone was basking in the joy and gratitude of having our brother back home to celebrate Christmas with us. We knew we would always refer to this day as "The time we had Christmas in January."

We had five more years to love, laugh, and celebrate with Terry and Laura. Terry was discharged from the Air Force, became a successful businessman active in his community, and was loved by all who knew him. He reveled in being a family man and an integral part of his loving extended family.

Sadly, we lost our brother in 1976, but Laura has become the fifth sister. That wonderful Christmas in January is one of our most cherished holiday memories.

49

Never Take Normal For Granted

At the age of thirty-five, I returned to school to become a nurse. Married with two children, I was dubbed non-traditional student. That was a kind way to say it wasn't normal.

When I was fourteen, I knew I wanted to be a nurse. Upon graduation from high school my life went in another direction. A few years later, I got married and had children. Never giving up on my dream, I prayed for a way to make it real. I started doing some research and gathering information.

One night at dinner, I shared my aspirations with the family. My husband thought I was out of my mind. Our two children, Margie, age fourteen, and Tim, seven, were in awe of my goal, not quite realizing how it would change their lives. I presented my well-researched plan while sharing my faith that God would show us how to manage school, children, a house, and a long daily commute.

Accepted into an excellent nursing program, I secured a student loan and was awarded a small scholarship. This undertaking meant long days and a fifty-two mile a day drive. Each family member had their jobs to do around the house to help out. The family was prepared. Barring any unforeseen glitches, we could do this.

In my second year of classes, three weeks into the semester, Tim broke his leg while playing soccer in the front yard. I can still see his contorted leg and hear his scream of pain and terror in my head. It definitely was not normal.

The ambulance took Tim to the hospital where I was training, twenty-six miles away. This proved to be a blessing.

With my tuition came a room in the nurse's residence which served as a place to quietly study or grab a quick nap. It made sense for me to stay there while Tim was confined to the hospital. When I wasn't in class or clinical, I was at Tim's bedside. After he fell asleep at night, I shuffled to my room in the residence hall, and tried to sleep. Every other night, I went home to have dinner with our daughter, Margie, while my husband went to the hospital. We were two ships passing in the night.

I was physically and mentally exhausted, yet somehow able to keep up with classes and required assignments. My instructors noticed. However, late in the afternoon one day, I fell asleep on my desk during lecture. One of my classmates caught the teacher looking in my direction and reached out to wake me. The instructor whispered, "Let her sleep. she's had a rough couple of days." As class was dismissed, I awoke having drooled over my textbook and my notes. For me, this was not normal.

After two weeks in traction, Tim was ready for a cumbersome cast called a hip spica. After the casting procedure, we were able to take him home.

It took two people to turn him every two hours to alternate pressure points on his bony prominences. I was amazed and grateful to find that we always had help.

Three months after the day of the accident, Tim had his cast removed and began a week of intense physical therapy to learn to walk again. He came home using a tiny walker, but soon progressed to crutches. At that point he was allowed to join his second grade classmates.

A kind neighbor drove Tim to and from school to eliminate his struggling with crutches on the bus. Margie supervised her younger brother after school and helped him with homework.

Soon, Tim was walking without assistance. I was still commuting each day to school in another city. A semblance of normal returned to our crazy routine.

I graduated two and a half years later, and made the Dean's List. The day of graduation, I created parchment diplomas for George, Margie, and Tim. Without their support, my dream would never have been realized. We will never take normal for granted.

50

Amorous Onyx

Onyx, our three-year-old black Labrador Retriever fell in love with an oversized inner tube on the lawn of our vacation home on the St. Lawrence River. Despite numerous commands to "heel," Onyx remained fixated on this black rubber object.

George tried again, "Onyx, heel!" The dog didn't seem to care. The situation was getting embarrassing.

Meanwhile, twenty-two other family members were either lounging in lawn chairs, floating on rafts in the water, or lying on towels on the grass. Noticing the ongoing power struggle between George and his love-struck dog, people made no effort to stifle giggles and guffaws.

One of my sisters came out of the house oblivious to the unfolding drama. Gail had just changed into her new black bathing suit and was preparing to spend some quiet time basking in the sun with the rest of us. She spread her beach towel on the grass and knelt to put down her book. Leaning forward on all fours she began to lower herself onto the towel. From my vantage point, I saw our dog bolt from the black inner tube to my black-suited sister.

"Oh no!" I exclaimed. I called out to my husband, "George, Grab Onyx!"

He sprinted across the lawn dodging sunbathers, water toys, and chaise lounges.

But, the dog was faster than her master. Onyx wrapped her front legs around my sister's waist and was, um, well, you know!

Watching the scene unfold before them, the rest of the family burst into belly-shaking laughter.

Gail screamed, "Get this dog off me!"

Disabled by hysteria, not one sister, brother-in-law, niece, or nephew ran to Gail's defense. Worse, no one captured the moment for all posterity.

My husband attempted to grab his dog. Onyx resisted George's efforts to disengage her. Gail screamed, Onyx smiled, and George was embarrassed. Eventually, my husband prevailed and led Onyx away.

Having memorably entertained the family, Onyx spent the rest of the afternoon in her kennel. Gail read her book in peace while basking in the afternoon sun.

About The Author

Nancy Panko is a retired pediatric RN and author of the award-winning novels *Sheltering Angels* and *Guiding Missal*. Nancy is a frequent contributor to *Chicken Soup for the Soul* books and is a member of the NC Scribes and The Military Writers Society of America. She has also published three award-winning children's books: *Blueberry Moose*, *Peachy Possums*, and *The Skunk Who Lost His Cents*. Her next endeavor is *If I Had a Baby Elephant...* Nancy Loves to be at the helm of their pontoon boat with her husband on beautiful Lake Gaston, North Carolina.

Made in the USA
Middletown, DE
10 August 2023

36318842R00096